Founding Fathers

A Play About the Writing of the Constitution

We the People

Article 1

Founding Fathers

A Play About the Writing of the Constitution

By William Tucker

Word Association Publishers
205 Fifth Avenue
Tarentum, Pennsylvania 15084

Printed in the United States of America.

ISBN: 1-932205-90-X
Library of Congress Control Number: applied for

Word Association Publishers
205 Fifth Avenue,
Tarentum, Pennsylvania 15084
www.wordassociation.com

Principle Characters

Ben Franklin
George Washington
James Madison
Alexander Hamilton
James Wilson
Gouverneur Morris
Mrs. House, a tavern keeper
Mr. Whately, a man of small means
Niles, a journeyman
Abraham, a journeyman
Coot, a frontiersman

Edmund Randolph (Virginia)
Oliver Ellsworth (Connecticut)
Roger Sherman (Connecticut)
Luther Martin   (Maryland)
Charles Pinckney (S. Carolina)
Mrs. Sterling
Mrs. Rittenhouse
Mrs. Ashcroft
Mrs. Blount
Mrs. Morris
Jared Phillips, a journalist

Cicero, a servant

The following delegates have minor roles that can be played in composite by a small group of actors.

Abraham Baldwin (Georgia)
Pierce Butler (South Carolina)
William Davie (North Carolina)
Nathaniel Gorham (Massachusetts)
Rufus King (Massachusetts)
William Patterson (New Jersey)
John Rutledge (South Carolina)
Hugh Williamson (North Carolina)
Charles Cotesworth Pinckney (South Carolina)
David Brearly (New Jersey)

Gunning Bedford, Jr. (Delaware)
George Clymer (Pennsylvania)
John Dickenson (Delaware)
William Johnson (Connecticut)
Robert Morris (Pennsylvania)
George Read (Delaware)
Richard Spaight (North Carolina)
George Wythe (Virginia)

Benjamin Franklin

New York Historical Society

Act One, Scene 1

Philadelphia, May 25, 1787, The City Tavern

Present are MRS. HOUSE, proprietor, and three patrons: NILES, a journeyman, COOT, a frontiersman, and MR. WHATELY, a man of some small means.

WHATELY: So I looked up the hill and saw this hat coming towards me. And I say to myself, "What on earth is that?"

MRS. HOUSE (cleaning the bar): Excuse me, Mr. Whately, could you move your arm just a bit there. Thank you. (She cleans past him.)

WHATELY: So it comes winding down the hill, left and right, until it stops right in front of me.

NILES: Rain like this, a man can sink up to his knees in mud.

WHATELY: Well that's exactly my point, don't you see? So I lifted up the hat to look under and there's the head of a friend of mine, Parson Brown.

(The door opens and ABRAHAM enters. Like Niles, he is a journeyman. He is covered with mud.)

ABRAHAM: Better get ready for company, Mrs. House. There's a gentleman outside whose horse turned lame.

MRS. HOUSE: A gentleman!

WHATELY: Yes, well if I could just finish . . .

MRS. HOUSE: Here's let's let Mr. Whately finish his story.

He's been trying to tell it all evening. (There is quiet.)

WHATELY: Well I picked up the hat and there was the head of my friend, Parson Brown. "A lot of mud we're having this year, isn't it Parson?" I say. "Can I be of any help to you?" And he replies . . .

COOT and ABRAHAM together: "No, that's alright, I've got a horse under me."

(All but Whately laugh. A gentleman enters. He is JAMES MADISON.)

COOT: I musta heerd that joke a thousand times.

MRS. HOUSE: (To Madison). Welcome, kind sir. Is there anything we can do to help you?

MADISON: Yes, madam. My name is James Madison. I've just ridden from Virginia. My horse has finally turned lame.

MRS. HOUSE: All the way from Virginia? My goodness. How long did it take you, Mr. Madison?

MADISON: About a week. I left last Friday.

MRS. HOUSE: Well here, let me get you some dry clothes. And have a drink. That will warm you up.

COOT: (continuing) I heerd that story in New Hampshire, where they got brown mud. I heerd it in Georgia, where they got red mud.

(Madison takes a seat, begins drying off.)

MRS. HOUSE: Terrible amount of mud we're having this year. (Hands him drink.) Here, take this. It'll warm you up. Cicero! (A black youth enters.) Take care of this gentleman's horse, will you?.

MADISON: If I could get in touch with Dr. Franklin . . . (The men exchange glances.)

MRS. HOUSE: We'll do that for you, don't worry.

(Mrs. House disappeared offstage with Cicero. The men are left together in an uneasy silence.)

ABRAHAM: Lot of rain we've been having this year, isn't it, sir?

MADISON: Indeed.

WHATELY: And mud! (Another uneasy silence.) I don't think I've ever seen such mud.

MADISON: You know that reminds me of something that happened, just as I was leaving home last week. I was going up the hill when I saw a hat coming toward me. Just a hat, slithering right along the ground, weaving a path, left and right, through the mud. (Motions.) Well, I got down and picked it up to look under and there was my friend . . . . ah, Farmer Jones, just his head, sticking out of the mud. "A lot of mud we're having this year, isn't it?" I said. "Sure is," he replied. "Is there anything I can do for you?" I asked. "No that's alright," he said, "I've got a horse under me!"

(All laugh uproariously.)

ABRAHAM: A horse under him!

WHATELY: Can you imagine?

3

NILES: Ain't that somethin'?

COOT: We ain't heard anything that funny around here in a long time.

MRS. HOUSE: (reentering) We certainly haven't! Now if you'll all just allow Mr. Madison –

ABRAHAM: Must be goin' to this convention they're havin', aren't you Mr. Madison?

MADISON: Yes I am.

WHATELY: Mr. Madison, are you by any chance acquainted with Mr. Thomas Jefferson, the author of our great Declaration of Independence?

MADISON: I am indeed, sir.

WHATELY: Do you now I once met Mr. Jefferson, right on the steps of the House of Burgesses -

COOT: A Son of Liberty, aren't you, Mr. Madison?

NILES: Fought at Trenton!

MADISON: No, I was a member of the Virginia Legislature . . .

ABRAHAM: Let's have a cheer for Mr. Madison!

ALL: Hip! Hip! Hooray!

WHATELY: Independence!

ALL: Hip! Hip! Hooray!

NILES: The Spirit of '76!

ALL: Hip! Hip! Hooray!

COOT: Fire a load of buckshot into old King George's britches and watch him run! (All laugh.)

ABRAHAM: Ah, them were the days, weren't they Mr. Madison?

MADISON: Indeed they were.

ABRAHAM: So what's this here convention supposed to be about?

MADISON: Well, we're trying to establish an orderly government so we won't have to -

WHATELY: It's preposterous, isn't it Mr. Madison. Armed men running around, trying to take over the country.

NILES: Them's farmers that lost their land.

WHATELY: But you can't . . . .

ABRAHAM: Ain't nobody gonna take my farm.

(Cicero reappears with another stranger. He is ALEXANDER HAMILTON.)

HAMILTON: Jemmy! My dear fellow. We heard you had some trouble.

MADISON: It's quite alright, Colonel Hamilton.

HAMILTON: Well, come to Dr. Franklin's. There's dinner waiting for you.

ABRAHAM: Excuse me sir. Is it Colonel *Alexander* Hamilton?

HAMILTON: (Stiffens a little.) That is correct.

ABRAHAM: I was with you at Yorktown, sir.

HAMILTON: Well, that's . . . . (extremely formal) very fine.

ABRAHAM: Pennsylvania volunteers, sir. We were on the north line, right next to the French command.

HAMILTON: That's very fine. (Shakes hands stiffly.)

ABRAHAM: It was a wonderful victory, sir. We didn't lose a man.

NILES: Here's to good old Yorktown!

WHATELY: And here's to Colonel Alexander Hamilton, George Washington's right-hand man!

ALL: Hip! Hip! Hooray!

HOUSE: Are you here for the meeting, sir?

HAMILTON: I am, madam.

HOUSE: What kind of government are you going to give us, sir?

HAMILTON: That's . . hard to say.

MADISON: We have no set purpose yet, madam. We're trying to revise the Articles of Confederation.

HAMILTON: Actually, we're here to see if a collection of thirteen squabbling principalities can be made into a nation.

COOT: There's only one question I want to ask, Colonel Hamilton. Will we keep our freedom?

HAMILTON: Freedom is a very elusive concept.

COOT: Well I been free all my life and it ain't been elusive to me.

HAMILTON: The amount of freedom a man can have usually depends on how much he can tolerate in others.

COOT: Well I don't know about others, but I can tolerate a whole lot. (Laughter)

ABRAHAM: Will George Washington be our leader, sir?

HAMILTON: There is every reason to believe General Washington will be part of the government.

NILES: If George Washington was our leader, the soldiers woulda been paid by now!

HAMILTON: Well, once Congress has been authorized to collect taxes -

NILES, ABRAHAM, and COOT: (A moment of astonishment.) TAXES!

HAMILTON: You can't have government without taxes.

ABRAHAM: But that's what we fought the war for, sir, to get rid of taxes.

HAMILTON: We fought against unjust taxation.

ABRAHAM: All taxes is unjust!

HOUSE: Sirs, I think we've borrowed enough of Mr. Hamilton and Mr. Madison's time. Your horses are ready, gentlemen. (To Cicero) Here, Cicero, help these gentleman with their baggage, will you?

WHATELY: May I be of any assistance to you gentlemen? I have many friends here in Philadelphia.

MADISON: That's alright, thank you sir.

HAMILTON: (To House) Thank you, madam.

HOUSE: Come again, gentlemen. Any time.

MADISON: Good night, madam. Good night, gentlemen.

ALL: Good night. Good night.

(Madison and Hamilton depart.)

WHATELY: James Madison and Alexander Hamilton. Isn't that extraordinary?

HOUSE: Quite a nice pair, aren't they?

ABRAHAM: That Colonel Hamilton's a bit standoffish.

WHATELY: Mr. Madison is quite diplomatic.

HOUSE: I wonder what kind of government they'll give us?

WHATELY: A republic! Just like Ancient Rome!

ABRAHAM: A democracy! No man better'n anyone else!

NILES: A gov'ment where the soldiers get paid, that's what I want!

COOT: I don't care what kind o' gov'ment they give us long as we keep our freedom!

+

Act I, Scene 2

Benjamin Franklin's study.

Present are BENJAMIN FRANKLIN, JAMES WILSON, and GOVERNOR EDMUND RANDOLPH. They have just finished a tour of Franklin's laboratory.

RANDOLPH: Thank you, Dr. Franklin, that was a wonderful experience.

FRANKLIN: I'm glad you enjoyed it, Governor Randolph.

RANDOLPH: You certainly have a marvelous laboratory.

FRANKLIN: I've a few small items of interest, Governor.

RANDOLPH: Now Doctor, don't be modest. Here you are a man who has stood up to kings and helped defeat the strongest army in the world, yet you've still never stopped pursuing the most wonderful scientific discoveries.

WILSON: (helping Franklin to be seated) Would you like me to get you a glass of water Doctor?

FRANKLIN: Yes, Mr. Wilson could you? (He and Randolph sit.) Well Governor, science is the application of human reason to the affairs of nature while politics is the application of reason to the affairs of men. So they aren't all that different.

RANDOLPH: I'm sorry, Doctor, I didn't mean to tire you.

FRANKLIN: That's quite alright, Governor. If a man can't indulge in the simple pleasures of conversation, he certainly doesn't have any business attending a gathering of the country's greatest political leaders, does he?

11

RANDOLPH: You're quite right, Doctor. Tell me, what do you think are the chances of saving our tottering system?

FRANKLIN: Oh, I've lived long enough to know that, while nothing is ever completely certain, nothing is altogether impossible either. We Americans are a practical people. We have republican virtue. The problem may be we have developed such an affection for overthrowing governments that we don't want to be governed by anyone, not even ourselves. (Wilson returns with a glass of water.) Thank you, Mr. Wilson.

RANDOLPH: That does seem to be the problem, doesn't it? Do you thing the delegates will be able to agree on anything?

FRANKLIN: Well, we can certainly agree on some things and we don't have to agree on everything. Often it is the little things that drive men apart while the big things draw them together.

RANDOLPH: Yes, I suppose that's true.

WILSON: The representation in Congress obviously needs revising. The idea of a few small states having veto power over the entire country is something most people find intolerable. (Randolph nods in agreement.)

FRANKLIN: Perhaps delegates such as yourselves from Pennsylvania or Virginia, Mr. Wilson, but I doubt whether Mr. Luther Martin of Maryland or Mr. Oliver Ellsworth of Connecticut find it intolerable.

RANDOLPH: Yes, I suppose that's right. Dr. Franklin, as you probably know, Mr. Madison and the Virginia delegates have asked me to present a proposal for reforming Congress. Is there any advice you can offer me?

FRANKLIN: I would suggest only that you make it simple, Governor Randolph. Think of Newton's explanation of the heavens. He looked at a world of apparent chaos and confusion and discovered in it an unseen balance of forces.

RANDOLPH: Exactly one hundred years ago, wasn't it? *The Principia?*

FRANKLIN: That's right, 1687.

WILSON: So a good system of government should also be held together by an unseen balance of forces.

RANDOLPH: Montesquieu's checks and balances!

FRANKLIN: Now you are turning philosopher on us, Mr. Wilson.

WILSON: By dividing government into the legislative, executive, and judicial branches, as Montesquieu suggests, we create a system that keeps competing factions in their place just as the planets are held in their orbits.

FRANKLIN: We do that, Mr. Wilson, but we also do what a good carpenter does when he creates a three-legged stool. He makes something that is useful without excess ornamentation.

RANDOLPH: So in setting up a government we must act as good carpenters.

FRANKLIN: We must *be* good carpenters, Governor Randolph. And in my experience it takes as much skill to be a good carpenter as it does to be a good statesman. Now shall we go inside, gentlemen? I think our little dinner is about to begin.

Act I, Scene 3

A dinner party at the home of Dr. Franklin, May 27, 1787.

Present are FRANKLIN, WILSON, RANDOLPH, GOUVERNEUR MORRIS, ALEXANDER HAMILTON, JAMES MADISON, GEORGE MASON, ROBERT MORRIS, OLIVER ELLSEWORTH, ROGER SHERMAN, CHARLES PINCKNEY, ELBRIDGE GERRY, JOHN DICKINSON, LUTHER MARTIN, RUFUS KING, and JOHN RUTLEDGE. They have just finished dinner. Franklin rises to speak.

FRANKLIN: Gentlemen. (Someone clinks glasses. Silence prevails.) Thank you very much. I hope you all enjoyed your dinner.

SEVERAL: Splendid. Wonderful.

FRANKLIN: Thank you. I will convey your complements to the cook. And now although we have very important matters before us, I'd like to begin by telling a little story. It's about a gallant knight who went off to the Crusades many, many years ago, leaving his poor wife, a rather handsome young wench, to pine alone. And although he trusted her virtue, just to make sure he took the precaution of leaving her wearing one of those . . . what do you call them?

GOUVERNEUR MORRIS: Chastity belt!

FRANKLIN: Yes, that's it. (General laughter.) Chastity belt. Well, he took this precaution, yet being a man of honor and considering he might meet his Maker on the battlefield, not wanting to condemn his poor wife to a life of abstinence, he was kind enough to leave her a key, in the hands of a young page.

15

Well he hadn't gotten very far when this page - a very strapping young fellow himself– came running after him. "Master, master," he says with some alarm, "Mistress tells me there must be some mistake. You've left the wrong key!"

(General appreciative laughter.)

KING: Are you sure this story didn't occur in South Carolina?

PINCKNEY: Dr. Franklin, I can vouch for the virtue of South Carolina women. We import all our chastity belts from Massachusetts.

KING: That's because we have no need for them!

(More laughter.)

RUTLEDGE: With all those cold nights, I'm not surprised.

FRANKLIN: Well, gentlemen, I tell this story because it deals with the matter of trust. You may recall my saying during the late War that we must all hang together or we would surly hang separately. Today I would say we must all hang together or we may soon be hanging each other. We face a task of forming a government for a people who might be just as content to live without one.

Now just to be sure we're all acquainted, let me go around the table and introduce everyone. To my right is Colonel Alexander Hamilton, certainly no stranger to you. (Hamilton stands and acknowledges polite applause.) Colonel Hamilton served under General Washington and has been instrumental in calling this convention.

To his right is Mr. Gouverneur Morris, (Morris stands) once a resident of New York, now residing here in Philadelphia, having left all his Tory sentiments on the banks of the Hudson.

MORRIS: Actually, sir, all I left there was my leg (slaps his wooden leg) and this one serves me just as well.

FRANKLIN: Next we have the honorable Edmund Randolph, Governor of Virginia. (Randolph stands and bows.) Also from Virginia Colonel George Mason, author of the Virginia Bill of Rights.

MASON: Dr. Franklin, we salute your efforts and I'm sure under the guidance of yourself and our beloved General George Washington, our deliberation cannot fail.

SEVERAL: Hear! Hear!

FRANKLIN: Next we have Mr. James Wilson, also of our fraternal city of Philadelphia. (WILSON stands.) Mr. Wilson is what we call a "Philadelphia lawyer," ready to lend his considerable oratorical skills to anything that lifts his conscience. (Murmur of laughter. A pregnant pause.)

KING: Or fills his purse!

(More laughter, Wilson acknowledges it.)

FRANKLIN: Now, gentlemen, although we tend to forget ourselves, our bodies always remind us of our age. And so I'm wondering if Mr. Wilson could kindly take over for me.

WILSON: Certainly, Dr. Franklin.

MASON: Pardon me, does anyone have a cigar?

HAMILTON: Here you are, sir. A very fine Jamaican cigar.

(A general hubbub as people exchange cigars.)

WILSON: (rapping for order). Gentlemen, let's finish up here. Next we have the Honorable Robert Morris, a signer of the Declaration of Independence who worked tirelessly to finance the Revolution. (Morris stands.) Mr. Oliver Ellsworth, a very fine jurist representing Connecticut in Congress. (Stands.) Mr. Roger Sherman, of Connecticut, also a signer of the Declaration.

SHERMAN: (Stands.) Thank you. And lest modesty make him forgetful, I should like to point out that Mr. Wilson himself was also a signer of our great Declaration. (Another round of applause.)

WILSON: Then we have Mr. James Madison, of Virginia, a rather young man who has been instrumental in calling this Convention. (Madison stands.) Mr. Charles Pinckney, a son of liberty representing South Carolina. (stands.) Mr. Pinckney, I believe your uncle, Charles Cotesworth Pinckney, will also be in attendance.

PINCKNEY: That is correct. In South Carolina, we think of politics as a family affair. (Laughter.)

WILSON: Mr. Elbridge Gerry, of Massachusetts, a Son of Liberty and signer of the Declaration of Independence. (Stands.) Mr. Rufus King, a very able young man, also from Massachusetts. Mr. Luther Martin, of Maryland, the honorable John Dickenson, of Delaware, and Mr. John Rutledge, of South Carolina, all of who will have important contributions to make. And then of course there is Dr. Franklin, with whom we are all familiar.

SEVERAL: Hear! Hear!

G. MORRIS: A toast to Fr. Franklin.

ALL: (rising) To Dr. Franklin! Hear! Hear!

WILSON: (When they are seated again) Gentlemen, there's no need to elaborate the difficulties that lie before us. Only last winter, 2,000 armed men trained in Worcester for four months before attempting to seize the Springfield Armory. Only the bitter weather and the heroic efforts of the Massachusetts militia prevented them from capturing the entire western portion of the state.

Gentlemen, the entire Continental Army never numbered more than 25,000. If rebellions similar to Shays' effort broke out in other states, could they not join forces? And if they did, is there any power on this continent that could keep them from seizing control of the government? Only three years ago Congress itself was routed from this very city by a ragtag band of soldiers from Valley Forge whose complaint was that they had not received three months wages. Does anyone believe this contemptible Congress that governs us could withstand a full-scale rebellion?

Gentlemen, the Confederation is an abject failure. It is nothing more than a treaty among thirteen independent states. Nine states have their own navies. Every state insists on coining its own money. And the Licentious Republic of Rhode Island is now printing paper money, which certainly means the end of civilization.

KING: "Rogue's Island!" (some laughter)

WILSON: Yes, this same Rogue's Island, with less than one-hundredth of the population, regularly brings the Confederacy to its knees by exercising its veto.

SEVERAL: Hear! Hear!

KING: It is my understanding that they have refused to send delegates to this convention.

ELLSWORTH: That is correct. (A murmur of disapproval.)

19

WILSON: Gentlemen, I won't belabor the point. We all stand for republican government. We want equal taxation with equal representation. Yet this artificial concept of "states" blinds us from our interest. We need a national government with national authority to carry out its own resolve. If we do not do something quickly we will find ourselves in what Mr. Hobbes has defined as the "State of Nature" – "the war of all against all."

(Sits down to long, sustained applause.)

G. MORRIS: I would like to second what Mr. Wilson has said. Gentlemen, the American people have what Mr. Montesquieu calls "republican virtue." They are capable of self-government. Right now their loyalties are turned to the states. But these sentiments will be fleeting. If we can build institutions worthy of respect, the people will embrace them. Time will do its work. The present generation, so fixed in its narrow state allegiances, will soon give way to a new generation of Americans.

SHERMAN: Yes, Mr. Wilson, I don't mean to interrupt, but may I pose a question?

WILSON: Certainly, Mr. Sherman.

SHERMAN: It is my understanding that we are here to consider amendments to the Articles of Confederation, is that correct?

WILSON: That is correct.

SHERMAN: Well, the Articles clearly state that no amendments may be adopted without the unanimous consent of the states. If, as we have heard here tonight, the State of Rhode Island has refused to send delegates, how is it possible we can do anything?

WILSON: (exasperated, looks at Madison): Mr. Madison?

MADISON: (rises) Let me begin by ceding Mr. Sherman's point.

The current Constitution does indeed require unanimous consent to undergo amendment. But I do not believe we should limit ourselves as to exactly what we are attempting to do over the next few weeks. We have been sent here by the states to consider the crisis before us. Any solutions we devise will be contingent on the states' approval. I think it would be best to proceed with the understanding that whatever we resolve here must later win the approval of the people.

MARTIN: The people or the states, Mr. Madison?

MADISON: Whatever the convention may determine.

MARTIN: (rising) Yes, excuse me Dr. Franklin, may I say a word? We've heard Mr. Wilson and Mr. Morris speak boldly of the need for a national government. Yet whence comes this mandate? When these colonies threw off the yoke of Britain, they did not surrender their rights to any national government. Nor are they prepared to make such a surrender today. When the people of Maryland think of good government then think of state government. Before the delegates start talking of a "national government," I would like to know whether anyone wants such a thing.

FRANKLIN: (rises) Yes, perhaps instead of presenting our individual agendas, we should try concentrating on those principles on which we can all agree.

DICKINSON: Yes, I'd like to agree, Dr. Franklin. One thing on which we are of one accord, I'm certain, is the rights of property. There is a very dangerous spirit abroad in the land today, a spirit of envy and leveling that tears down ancient laws and privileges. In paraphrasing Mr. Locke, our beloved Mr. Jefferson - who is in Paris, I believe?

WILSON: Mr. Jefferson is in Paris representing our government, as is Mr. John Adams? (Looks for assistance.)

21

KING: Mr. Adams is in England at the Court of St. James. He will not be attending the convention. However, he has written a wonderful book on Constitutional government that I would recommend to all of you.

DICKINSON: Yes, well, Mr. Jefferson, in paraphrasing Mr. Locke's phrase of "Life, Liberty, and Property," has written that we are all guaranteed the rights of "life, liberty, and the pursuit of happiness." Now I think all of us can agree that the right to happiness must include the right to hold and defend property. Without this guarantee, our civilization will quickly degenerate into a war of all against all, as the events in Massachusetts so clearly illustrate.

HAMILTON: Yes, I would like to second Mr. Dickinson. Gentlemen, in the short time of our independence, all of us have been amazed at the violence of the democratic spirit. Whatever great object is pursued by the people, it spreads like wildfire. Paper money, the cancellation of debts, breach of contract - whatever seizes the popular passion becomes irresistible in the state legislatures.

What can be done to tame these passions? Very little. Give all power to the many and they will oppress the few. Give power to the few and they will oppress the many. The only reasonable alternative, I believe, is to give power to men of virtue. A strong Senate on the Roman model, a strong executive, perhaps based on the constitutional monarchs of Europe - these are possibilities we may have to consider.

WILSON: Mr. Ellsworth?

ELLSWORTH: I must return to the comments of my colleagues, Mr. Sherman and Mr. Martin of Maryland, in asking whence comes this mandate for national government? If, as Mr. Dickenson and Col. Hamilton have suggested, the state governments have been such poor protectors of property, how, may I ask, can we expect any better from a powerful national government? Each state may be plagued with its own demagogues, but what will happen when all these feckless leaders are assembled in one place? Can we expect any better? Or will we only be creating something worse?

WILSON: (A bit nonplussed.) Mr. Madison, perhaps you could help us again?

MADISON: (barely audible) Yes, Mr. Wilson. I admit the problem Mr. Ellsworth has mentioned. But I think in time we may be able to resolve it. In preparation for this convention I have spent much time reading the history of republican government. It is a melancholy epic. The pages of history are littered with their bones. Each of these experiments was carried out in a city no broader than a day's walk, yet each failed ignominiously. Why? Republican government quickly leads to democracy and democracy leads to mob rule. Once the mob wins control, it turns on the owners of property to the impoverishment of all. Lacking the basic necessities, the people vest all power in a tyrant and liberty soon perishes of its own excesses.

If liberty cannot survive on so small a scale, what conceit allows us to think it can take root in a territory as vast as our own?

Upon further reflection, however, I have concluded the very vastness of our territory may actually work to our advantage. First, although unworthy men often gain sway in small communities, our larger territory may produce a sifting process whereby only the better sort of men gain national prominence. Second, as a republic embraces greater territory, the chance that any one faction may gain sway diminishes. We are more likely to have majorities formed out of negotiation and compromise. Thus, the very magnitude of the task before us may ultimately work to our benefit. The American people already have the habit of self-government. More than a century of administering our own affairs has made us essentially self-sufficient. It may be necessary only to sustain this wisdom and self-confidence in order to achieve our task.

(Sits down to sustained applause.)

FRANKLIN: Thank you, Mr. Madison. It always astonishes me that someone less than half my age can know more than I could ever hope to learn in several lifetimes.

Gentlemen, I sometimes wonder if the American people haven't developed a greater taste for overthrowing governments than for living under them. The kings and princes of Europe are bemused at our efforts, knowing that failure on our part will condemn the world to generations more of autocratic government. Yet I think we have reason to be confident. Ours has been a blessed generation. We have already seen the overthrow of a tyranny that seemed beyond all reform. Now we can see the beginnings, at least, of an experiment in self-government that is unparalleled in the pages of history. As we come together in calm deliberation to correct the flaws we have discovered in this experiment, let us pray that a benign Providence will once again smile upon our efforts.

Thank you for your attendance, gentlemen, and I look forward to seeing you at the State House tomorrow.

(Scattering of applause as party breaks up.)

Act I, Scene 4

Independence Hall, May 28, 1787.

The Convention is in full assembly.

CHAIRMAN GEORGE WYTHE: (banging gavel) Gentlemen! Gentlemen! May we have it quiet please? You have heard the proposed rules of the convention. Are there any questions?

RUTLEDGE: Mr. Chairman, will it be permitted to keep notes or journals during the debate?

WYETH: (Consults for a moment.) Members will be allowed to keep a journal only with permission of the chair. Nothing spoken in this house shall be printed, published, or communicated with any member of the public. Most important, there shall be no communications with any journalists or other members of the scribbling trade.

ROBERT MORRIS: Mr. Chairman, I would like to present a letter from sundry persons in the State of Rhode Island. They have informed us they will not be attending the convention.

(A murmur of disapproval.)

CHAIRMAN WYTHE: Is there any further business? Alright, the chair will accept nominations for President of this convention.

ROBERT MORRIS: Mr. Chairman, on behalf of the delegation from Pennsylvania, I would like to nominate George Washington, Esquire, late commander in chief of the American Armies, for president of this convention.

RUTLEDGE: Mr. Chairman, on behalf of South Carolina, I second the motion. Further, I would move that the choice of the delegates be unanimous.

WYTHE: All in favor?

ALL: AYE!

(Morris and Rutledge escort WASHINGTON to the chair amid loud applause.)

WASHINGTON: Thank you my fellow delegates. I must remind you of the novelty of these responsibilities for someone of my background. I beg the indulgence of the House toward any involuntary errors I may make.

Gentlemen, I need hardly remind you of the gravity of our task. We have been charged by the people with finding a satisfactory course for the future of our nation. Our disagreements may be numerable, but our mutual interest is plain.

It is all too common in history that such disagreements were decided by the sword. Yet we are met here today in calm deliberation to try to avoid such an outcome. Let us be restrained and enlightened in our discussions.

There is no guarantee of our success. It is altogether possible that no plan we propose here will win the consent of the majority. Yet if, to please the people, we offer something that we ourselves cannot approve, how can we afterwards defend our work? Let us raise, then, a standard to which the wise and honest can repair. The rest is in the hand of God.

Is there any further business? (No response.) Then we shall adjourn until tomorrow, at which time Governor Randolph has requested the floor.

(Meeting adjourns.)

Act II, Scene 1

A reception at the home of Robert Morris. May 29, 1787.

About two-dozen men and women mingle on stage. In the background, GEORGE and MARTHA WASHINGTON stand, shaking hands with visitors. In the foreground are MRS. MORRIS, MRS. STERLING, MRS. RITTENHOUSE, and GOVERNOR RANDOLPH.

STERLING: Governor, I heard you gave a wonderful speech at the convention today.

RANDOLPH: It was tolerably good, madam.

RITTENHOUSE: Isn't it exciting to be participating in all this, Governor? Aren't you thrilled?

MRS. MORRIS: Makes one feel like a part of history, doesn't it?

RANDOLPH: Indeed it does, madam.

STERLING: Could you give us a hint of what you said, Governor. Just so we can gossip a bit?

RANDOLPH: Madam, as you know, the delegates are pledged to secrecy.

STERLING: Yes, of course, Governor, we know that well. Just a smidgen, though, so we can have some inkling of what's going on.

MORRIS: We won't understand it anyway, Governor.

RITTENHOUSE: And we won't breathe a word!

RANDOLPH: Good ladies, I appreciate your curiosity. And although I am pledged to secrecy, in honor of your beauty and charm, I will reveal just a faint suggestion of my thoughts.

RITTENHOUSE: Just a whisper, Governor.

STERLING: So we won't have to guess.

RANDOLPH: (Conspiratorially.) Well, good ladies, I perceive our current misfortune to the fault of Congress. (They all nod.) It is entirely too weak and ineffectual. What I have proposed instead is to replace it with a national legislature made of two branches, an assembly elected by the people and a higher branch - the senate - elected by the assembly.

STERLING: That's just like they had in ancient Rome, isn't it, Governor?

RITTENHOUSE: Cicero and Julius Caesar and all that.

RANDOLPH: Precisely.

MORRIS: Sounds most promising.

RITTENHOUSE: I should say.

STERLING: But didn't Rome fall, Governor?

RANDOLPH: Well, yes, I suppose that's true.

MORRIS: Yes, that's right. Rome did fall, didn't it.

RITTENHOUSE: The Visigoths and Ostrogoths and all that.

STERLING: So how would we avoid a similar fate?

RANDOLPH: Well, ah . . . I don't...Well, ah, Mr. Gibbon, in his recent book, which I'm sure you've read.

STERLING: The first volume, at least.

RANDOLPH: Yes, well, ah, Mr. Gibbon, I believe, attributes the Fall of Rome to, ah . . . . Christianity.

RITTENHOUSE: Christianity!

MORRIS: How could that be?

STERLING: But we're a Christian country, aren't we Governor!

RANDOLPH: Yes, well, I suppose that's true.

STERLING: So how would we avoid that?

RANDOLPH: (stumped) Well, ah . . . we'll have to find a way around it, I guess.

MORRIS: That's a shame.

RITTENHOUSE: Governor, I think when Mr. Gibbon speaks of Christianity he was referring to the more primitive varieties, wasn't he?

RANDOLPH: Yes, I suppose that's right.

MRS. MORRIS: Like the Anabaptists.

RITTENHOUSE: Or the Millennialists.

STERLING: The Shakers!

RANDOLPH: Oh, you ladies are teasing me.

STERLING: Nonsense, Governor. It is you who are teasing us!

RANDOLPH: (Regaining strength) No, as I understand it, Rome began to fall when Julius Caesar was assassinated on the floor of the Senate.

RITTENHOUSE: That was Brutus, wasn't it?

MORRIS: Yes, Shakespeare talks about it.

RITTENHOUSE: (draws an imaginary dagger) *Et tu, Brute?* (They all laugh.)

STERLING: You know I saw the most wonderful production of that in Paris last year.

RANDOLPH: In English or in French, madam?

STERLING: Mais en francais, bien sure.

(All laugh again.)

MORRIS: I wish my French were that good.

RITTENHOUSE: Oh don't let Madame Sterling fool you. She just came from her tutor.

RANDOLPH: You know they say it's all true, what happened in those Shakespeare plays.

STERLING: Well, there's a bit of art in there somewhere, I'll warrant.

RANDOLPH: Madam?

STERLING: "The Tempest," I suspect, has some imagination.

RITTENHOUSE: He means the histories, dear Madam Sterling. Henry IV and Henry V and all that.

MORRIS: There really was a Macbeth. I read that somewhere.

RANDOLPH: The thing that puzzles me, though, is the way they talked back in those old days. All those rhymes and everything. I confess I can hardly understand a word they're saying.

MORRIS: "Shakespeare's woodnotes wild!" Didn't someone say that?

STERLING: Dr. Johnson finds him quite barbaric.

RITTENHOUSE: You're not talking in rhymes at this convention, are you dear Governor?

RANDOLPH: I should say not - we'd never get anything done, would we?

STERLING: Yes, supposed this were a play and we were all talking in verse? Wouldn't that be something? Here, let's give it a try.

Our noted Governor Randolph here today
        Must tell us . . . . .

RITTENHOUSE: . . . . how our country's future stands.

STERLING: And if . . .

RITTENHOUSE: . . . . from this convention . .   .

BOTH: . . . . . he's attending

RITTENHOUSE: We'll have .   .   .   .

BOTH: .   .   .   a da-da, da-da, da-da, da.

(All laugh.)

RANDOLPH: It's much too difficult, ladies.

RITTENHOUSE: You must be our Shakespeare, Governor.

RANDOLPH: Oh, nonsense, I'd never -

STERLING: Anyway, Governor, you were saying something about Rome, weren't you?

RITTENHOUSE: Yes, the Senate.

(HAMILTON and MADISON approach.)

RANDOLPH: Yes, well . . . .

RITTENHOUSE: Colonel Hamilton, how nice to see you.

HAMILTON: (He bows.) Madam.

RITTENHOUSE: Governor Randolph has just been giving us a little lecture on Rome.

STERLING: Telling us when in Rome to do as the Romans do.

(All laugh.)

HAMILTON: I'm sure Governor Randolph is eminently qualified to speak on such matters. (Something passes between him and Randolph.)

RITTENHOUSE: Anyway, Governor, speaking of Julius Caesar, do you suppose our own General Washington can compare with such men?

MRS. MORRIS: He does cut a magnificent figure, doesn't he?

STERLING: He's gone quite gray, though, hasn't he?

MORRIS: Madame Sterling!

STERLING: No, I don't mean it unkindly. I think it becomes him.

RANDOLPH: You know it's funny you should say that, madam. You know, of course, the story of the mutiny in Newburgh, where the General was forced to put down a rebellion among his own troops?

RITTENHOUSE: We hadn't heard of it, Governor.

RANDOLPH: It was only four years ago, when the army was still camped on the Hudson. The soldiers hadn't been paid in six months and were in a terrible mood - of course many of them still haven't been paid, but then they were all in one place. Anyway, someone - I believe it was old Horatio Gates - circulated a petition urging the soldiers to march on Philadelphia.

MORRIS: How dreadful!

RITTENHOUSE: That would have been dangerous.

RANDOLPH: Well, Washington got word and surprised everyone by coming to the meeting. It was quite awful. The soldiers would not be mollified. He gave a short speech telling them they were betraying the whole noble effort yet still they remained rebellious.

For one long, horrible instant, it appeared the General had lost control of his own army. Then at last he pulled from out of his pocket a letter from Congress promising they would be paid shortly. He held it before him, moving it back and forth, until it became obvious he could not read it. A hush fell over the assembly. Then, with all eyes upon him, General Washington did something I had never seen him do before. He reached into his breast pocket and pulled out a pair of spectacles. "Gentlemen, you must forgive me," he said. "Not only have I grown gray but I find I have gone nearly blind in the service of my country."

There was not a dry eye in the room. Officers and soldiers wept openly. The rebellion dissolved. It may be for this reason alone that we are not living under a military despotism today.

(A moment of silent appreciation.)

MORRIS: I had no idea.

RITTENHOUSE: So we have General Washington to thank for this.

RANDOLPH: Nor are we out of the woods entirely, madam.

HAMILTON: He is our modern Cincinnatus, madam. Not since Rome has a military leader surrendered his sword for the sake of his country.

STERLING: Which reminds me, Governor, you were telling us about Rome . . .

HAMILTON: Good ladies, I am going to excuse myself.

ALL: Good night, Colonel Hamilton.

STERLING: Now Governor, about this Senate . . . .

(Hamilton and Madison move aside. GOUVERNEUR MORRIS joins them.)

MORRIS: Quite a bevy of beauties our good Governor has collected, isn't it?

HAMILTON: He is regaling them with state secrets.

MORRIS: You mean the famous Randolph plan?

HAMILTON: He could at least have the decency to tell them Jemmy wrote it for him.

MORRIS: So that was your little effort, Mr. Madison?

MADISON: I apologize for its timidity, Mr. Morris. I'm afraid it's all the delegates will countenance now.

MORRIS: No, no, it was quite good for a start, Mr. Madison, quite good. We'll eventually want something stronger.

(GENERAL CHARLES COTESWORTH PINCKNEY approaches.)

PINCKNEY: Mr. Morris, Mr. Madison, Colonel Hamilton, nice to see you.

MORRIS: Our pleasure, General.

PINCKNEY: (Surveying the room.) An extraordinarily beautiful home Mr. Morris has here, isn't it?

HAMILTON: Indeed it is, General.

MORRIS: Have you anything like it in South Carolina, General?

PINCKNEY: Oh, we can hold our own, Mr. Morris. Charleston is a small city but we are developing our own architectural style.

HAMILTON: It is a splendid City, General. Second only to Philadelphia.

PINCKNEY: Have you been through the line to meet General Washington yet?

MORRIS: Oh, the General and I are long acquainted.

PINCKNEY: An extraordinary man, isn't he? Something very ancient in those eyes.

HAMILTON: Indeed there is.

PINCKNEY: So do you think we'll get a government out of this, gentlemen?

MORRIS: We shall see, General. We shall see.

Act II, Scene 2

The Convention Floor, June 4, 1787.

The Convention has dissolved itself into a Committee of the Whole, so that any votes taken are not binding. This format continues until September. DR. NATHANIEL GORHAM, of Massachusetts, who at the time was President of Congress, presides over the Committee.

DR. GORHAM: The motion on the floor is Governor Randolph's resolution number four, "that the members of the first branch of the National Legislature ought to be elected by the people of the several states." Any discussion?

SHERMAN: Mr. Chairman, I oppose this resolution and would suggest election by the state legislatures. The people should have as little immediate say about the government as possible. They tend to want information and are constantly being misled.

GERRY: Mr. Chairman, I would agree. The evils we now experience flow from an excess of democracy. In Massachusetts, the people are daily misled into the most baneful measures by false reports from pretended patriots. At this very moment there is a popular clamor to lower the salaries of public officials and abolish taxes altogether. I must admit I have been a republican in spirit, but experience has taught me the danger of this leveling spirit of democracy.

MASON: Mr. Chairman, I must take strong exception to the gentleman from Massachusetts. The Legislature is the grand repository of the democratic principle of government. It will be our House of Commons. Therefore it ought to be known and sympathized with in every part of the community. I admit we may have been too democratic over the last few years, but I am afraid lest we should run to the opposite extreme and lose popular support altogether.

WILSON: Mr. Chairman, I concur with Colonel Mason. I am for raising the federal pyramid to a considerable altitude. But for that reason, I would like to give it as broad a base as possible.

GERRY: Mr. Chairman, I remain opposed to popular election. However, I have no objections if men of honor and character might be willing to accept appointment.

HAMILTON: Call the question, Mr. Chairman.

GORHAM: Roll call on the question, "All members of the first branch of the Legislature shall be elected by the people."

ROLL CALL: MASS: Aye. CONN. Divided. NEW YORK: Aye. NEW JERSEY: No. PENNSYLVNIA: Aye. MARYLAND: Divided. DELAWARE: Divided. NORTH CAROLINA: Aye. SOUTH CAROLINA: Aye. GEORGIA: Aye.

GORHAM: The motion carries, seven in favor, one opposed, three divided.

(A long burst of sustained applause.)

GORHAM: We will now consider resolution number five: "that the second, or `senatorial' branch ought to be chosen by the first branch, with candidates nominated by the state legislatures."

SPAIGHT: Mr. Chairman, I contend that the members of the Senate ought to be chosen directly by Members of the state legislatures and move to that effect.

BUTLER: I must agree. I think we are being altogether too quick in taking power out of the hands of the states. We are destroying the balance of interests that we should be preserving.

WILSON: Mr. Chairman, I am opposed to election of senators by either the state legislatures or the first branch of Congress. I think we should draw election districts throughout the country based on equal population.

MADISON: Mr. Chairman, unfortunately I believe Mr. Wilson's proposal would destroy the influence of the smaller states.

PINCKNEY: Call the question, Mr. Chairman, on whether the members of the Second House shall be elected by the First House on nominations from the state legislatures.

SHERMAN: Seconded.

GORHAM: All in favor of the resolution? (None.) Opposed?

ALL: Nay!

GORHAM: The motion fails. Let us adjourn until tomorrow when we shall once again take up the question of representation in the Senate. I would ask the members not to be discouraged by this vote, however. Taken altogether, we are making progress.

Act II, Scene 3

A reception at the home of Mrs. Rittenhouse. June 7, 1787.

MRS. RITTENHOUSE, MRS. STERLING, MRS. ASHCROFT, MRS. BLOUNT, ROGER SHERMAN, OLIVER ELLSWORTH, and JAMES WILSON in conversation.

ELLSWORTH: Will you be in Philadelphia all summer, madam?

RITTENHOUSE: What, and miss the chance to see these extraordinary events? Why certainly, Mr. Ellsworth.

SHERMAN: Have you visited our part of the country, madam?

RITTENHOUSE: Connecticut? No I haven't.

SHERMAN: It's quite beautiful.

ELLSWORTH: Have any of you ladies ever visited our Western Reserve, Madam?

RITTENHOUSE: Where is that, Mr. Ellsworth?

ELLSWORTH: Just west of Pennsylvania.

STERLING: Isn't that the land you were trying to steal from us recently?

SHERMAN: On the contrary, it was our impression that you were stealing it from us.

BLOUNT: But isn't that part of Pennsylvania, Mr. Sherman?

SHERMAN: Connecticut's royal charter clearly gives us title to that part of the Northwest Territories in the Ohio Valley.

STERLING: But why do you need land way out there, there Mr. Sherman?

ELLSWORTH: We have no room to expand, madam. New York is to our west, Massachusetts on our north, our people have no place to go.

RITTENHOUSE: Come to Philadelphia, Mr. Ellsworth. We've plenty of room for you here.

ASHCROFT: Yes, we're all Americans, aren't we?

SHERMAN: Well, that's certainly true in one sense, madam. But there are other considerations.

BLOUNT: Such as . . .

SHERMAN: The states must pay their war debts. We're hoping to meet our obligations.

WILSON: The federal government is also in debt, madam. We are borrowing just to pay interest.

(The ladies look befuddled.)

BLOUNT: So what has this to do with the Western Reserve, gentlemen?

ELLSWORTH: Both the state and federal governments hope to sell that land to retire their debt, madam.

SHERMAN: There's a question of whose claim shall prevail.

RITTENHOUSE: But isn't this exactly the kind of tug-of-war that is dividing us, Mr. Ellsworth?

ELLSWORTH: The people remain very attached to their states, madam. They don't want all their affairs administered here in Philadelphia.

STERLING: Yes, but we're all Americans, Mr. Ellsworth! Don't you think of yourself as an American, Mr. Wilson?

WILSON: I do, madam, although others may not share my view.

ELLSWORTH: Now Mr. Wilson, you know that's not fair. I think of myself as an American just as much as you do.

MRS. BLOUNT: Doesn't General Washington own land out there in the West somewhere?

WILSON: The General's holdings are in Kentucky, madam. They are not under dispute.

STERLING: Are you suggesting that other delegates have land that is under dispute?

SHERMAN: There are instances, madam.

MRS. BLOUNT: Does Col. Hamilton own land somewhere, Mr. Sherman?

ELLSWORTH: Col. Hamilton's interest runs to power, madam, not land.

(All laugh.)

MRS. BLOUNT: So who will eventually decide all this, Mr. Ellsworth?

ELLSWORTH: I believe that is one of the issues under consideration at this Convention.

STERLING: Such important concerns. Are there any other such crucial issues dividing us?

(An embarrassed look around.)

SHERMAN: Well, there's the question of the war debt, madam.

ASHCROFT: And what might that involve, Mr. Sherman?

WILSON: There are approximately $30 million in unfunded securities floating around - money loaned to the government by individuals during the war.

STERLING: And . . . .

WILSON: Without a national government, there's very little chance these debts will ever be paid.

BLOUNT: So?

SHERMAN: Well, I myself have only a small holding, but . . . I believe some of the delegates are . . . . rather heavily committed.

ASHCROFT: Well isn't that interesting?

STERLING: Now we get to the bottom of things.

RITTENHOUSE: And can we assume, gentlemen, that the delegates can put such personal matters aside as they deliberate things this summer?

SHERMAN: We hope so, madam. We hope so.

Act II, Scene 4

The Convention Floor, June 13

GORHAM: The matter before the floor is resolution 7, "that a national executive be instituted, to be chosen by the legislature, for (blank) years in office."

WILSON: Mr. Chairman, I would move that the position of the executive be held by a single individual.

PINCKNEY: Seconded.

(There is a moment of embarrassment in which everyone becomes acutely aware of WASHINGTON'S presence.)

FRANKLIN: (rising to the occasion) Yes, Mr. Chairman, although we are all fairly certain of the qualities we would be looking for in such an individual, perhaps before we vote it would be well if some of the gentlemen delivered their sentiments on some of the more general questions relating to this office.

RUTLEDGE: Yes, there is no reason to be shy in discussing this matter. For my opinion, I believe a single executive would be the best. But I am not for giving him powers of war and peace. These should be reserved for the legislature.

PINCKNEY: Yes, Mr. Chairman, I am for a vigorous executive but am also afraid that extending the powers of war and peace would render this individual not only a monarch but the very worst kind, an elected one.

SHERMAN: Mr. Chairman, this executive magistrate is nothing more than an institution for carrying out the will of the legislature. Therefore, I think the legislature itself should decide whether to appoint one or more executives.

RANDOLPH: Mr. Chairman, I too strenuously oppose a single executive. The fixed genius of the American people requires that we wean ourselves from the British model. I believe the requisites of vigor, dispatch, and responsibility can be found in three men as easily as one.

MADISON: Mr. Chairman, perhaps before we settle this point we could discuss how the executive is to be elected and the length of his term.

(A general murmur of consent.)

WILSON: Mr. Chairman, I would suggest election by the people. The experience in both New York and Massachusetts has shown that this is the most successful mode.

SHERMAN: Mr. Chairman, I am for appointment by the legislature. An executive independent of the legislature will quickly become the essence of a tyranny.

(A moment of embarrassment over these disagreements.)

MADISON: Mr. Chairman, perhaps we could agree on the term of office. I move that the executive serve for three years with the assumption of re-eligibility.

PINCKNEY: I move seven years with no re-eligibility for office, Mr. Chairman.

BREARLY: Seconded.

SHERMAN: I move three years and against the doctrine of rotation. If we are continually changing the office, we will be throwing out the most qualified men.

BEDFORD: Mr. Chairman, I am against election for seven years. What will happen if the magistrate proves to lack the proper qualifications? I am for election every three years with eligibility for three terms.

HAMILTON: Call the question on election for seven years, Mr. Chairman.

MORRIS: Seconded.

ROLL CALL: MASS: divided; CONN: no; N.Y.: aye; N.J.: aye; PENN: aye; DEL: aye; MD: divided; VIRG: aye; N.C.: no; S.C.: no; GA: no.

SECRETARY: The committee divides five aye, four, no, two divided.

MORRIS: Could we have a ruling from the chair on whether the motion passes?

GORHAM: (after a moment on consultation) The chair rules a plurality is sufficient to carry the vote. The motion for a seven-year term is adopted. The chair now recognizes Dr. Franklin.

FRANKLIN: Mr. Chairman, could I add a word to this discussion? I would move that the following phrase be added, "that the executive's necessary expenses shall be defrayed, but that he not receive a salary or other reward for his services."

Men seek office for power or profit. When the two are combined, the chances grow that the office will attract men in search of too much power. Therefore I suggest that our executive work without remuneration. This may seem Utopian, but consider the humble Quakers of Pennsylvania. They resolve all controversies at monthly meetings and there is no compensation offered. Yet they never lack for volunteers.

HAMILTON: Mr. Chairman, may I request the honor of seconding Dr. Franklin's motion? May I also move that we table it to give the delegates time to ruminate over his remarks?

WILSON: Seconded.

ALL: Aye.

PATTERSON: Mr. Chairman, may I also move that we table this entire discussion of the executive and return to the matter of representation in the Senate? I make this recommendation because I consider representation by population alone as striking at the very existence of the lesser states. The people of America are sharp-eyed. They will not be deceived that we are here only amending the Articles of Confederation. In fact, what we are setting a course for is an entirely unprecedented form of national government.

BREARLY: I would like to second the motion. There are three large states - Massachusetts, Pennsylvania, and Virginia. It does not take much examination to see that in such a legislature these states will carry all before them while minor states such as New York and Delaware will be swept aside.

WILSON: Mr. Chairman, I cannot understand this view that says people belong to states before they belong to the nation. Is a citizen of Delaware diminished by saying he is a citizen of the United States? Shall it take 150 of my fellow constituents in Pennsylvania to balance 50 constituents of Mr. Patterson in New Jersey? If the small states will not conform to Mr. Randolph's plan, then I must inform Mr. Patterson that the larger states will not conform to any other.

PATTERSON: Mr. Chairman, speaking as a representative of New Jersey, I can tell you my constituents will never confederate on the plan now before this committee. I would rather submit to a monarch than to a plan where three states have their will and the rest catch as catch can.

FRANKLIN: Gentlemen! Gentlemen! May I remind you that we are sent here to *consult* each other, not to *contend* with each other. Declarations of fixed opinion will neither enlighten nor convince anyone. Positiveness and warmth on one side naturally beget their like on the other. For myself, I cannot see what advantage the greater states could gain by swallowing the smaller ones, except perhaps a case of indigestion. If the delegates remain bound to their local interest, however, I would suggest a third alternative where the states are represented by the amount of money they put into the national treasury.

HAMILTON: Mr. Chairman, in view of the many proposals put before this body today, I would move that we adjourn now so the delegates can give these matters some thought.

PATTERSON: I second the motion. But I would like to reserve the floor tomorrow for the presentation of another plan that will better represent the interests of New Jersey and the other smaller states.

GORHAM: Very well, let us adjourn. Mr. Patterson will have the floor when we return tomorrow.

George Washingon

New York Historical Society

James Madison

New York Historical Society

Alexander Hamilton

New York Historical Society

Govenor Morris

New York Historical Society

James Wilson by Philip Fisbourne Wharton, after the James Barton Longacre.
Engraving from a painting by Jea Pierre Henri Elouis, 1873

Independence National Historical Park

Act II, Scene 5

A reception at Mrs. Blount's house. June 15, 1787

MRS. STERLING and GENERAL PINCKNEY in the foreground.

STERLING: So what do you think of Mr. Patterson's proposal, General Pinckney?

PINCKNEY: Madam, I am amazed at your intelligence. Are you a little church mouse that can hide in the rafters?

STERLING: Come now, General, you know I wouldn't think of eavesdropping on your deliberations.

PINCKNEY: Or perhaps you have disguised yourself as a sentry so you can gain admittance?

STERLING: Are you saying a man of your qualities couldn't discern a woman's form in the disguise of a soldier, General?

PINCKNEY: I graciously cede the point, madam.

STERLING: So what do think of Mr. Patterson's proposal?

PINCKNEY: Madam, since it appears there is no trust here that has not already been broken.

(They begin to draw together.)

STERLING: Once lost, a woman's honor can never be restored, General.

PINCKNEY: Yes, I understand, madam. So, on this very delicate matter of state. . . .

STERLING: The honorable state of . . . . New Jersey.

(GOVERNOR RANDOLPH approaches.)

RANDOLPH: Oh, I'm sorry, I didn't mean to interrupt anything.

STERLING: Not at all, Governor. We were just talking . . . politics.

PINCKNEY: New Jersey, as a matter of fact.

RANDOLPH: Oh, the good Mr. Patterson's proposal. Brought us full circle, wouldn't you say, General? Right back to the old Confederacy. In my opinion - (to Sterling) Excuse me, madam, the General and I will just talk privately here a moment.

STERLING: Go ahead, I won't listen. (She listens.)

RANDOLPH: In my opinion, it's just a matter of self-interest. Give New Jersey an equal vote and she will confederate. Vote by population and she will cut adrift.

(GEORGE MASON and MRS. RITTENHOUSE have approached as he speaks.)

MASON: Yes, I quite agree, Governor. The sentiments of the American people are entirely attached to two houses of the legislature. Does Mr. Patterson seriously think we shall surrender both sword and purse to a single house where each state has but one vote?

RITTENHOUSE: But the small states like Delaware and New Jersey, Colonel Mason, don't they fear being reduced to insignificance?

(JAMES WILSON has also approached.)

WILSON: They are already reduced to insignificance, madam. There's nothing can be done about it. Giving them inordinate power can only frustrate the will of the majority.

(As they talk, MADISON, HAMILTON, and GOU-VERNEUR MORRIS have gathered around.)

MORRIS: Don't worry, madam. Our resident genius, Mr. Madison, is working on a solution to the problem at this very moment.

RITTENHOUSE: Oh, how exciting. Tell us Mr. Madison, what do you think?

MADISON: (extremely embarrassed). Madam, I don't know whether I'm allowed to break my vows of secrecy.

RITTENHOUSE: Oh, that's alright, Mr. Madison. Everyone else is talking.

MADISON: (reluctantly) Yes, but . . . . well, I will say that, in the long run, this concern over the large and small states will not be our most serious difficulty.

RITTENHOUSE: You don't think there's cause for concern, Mr. Madison?

STERLING: Yes, what could be more serious, Mr. Madison?

MADISON: (extremely embarrassed) I don't think I'm at liberty to say, madam.

RITTENHOUSE: Oh come now, Mr. Madison, you're among friends. (There is a general consent he should speak his mind.)

STERLING: Yes, tell us your thoughts, Mr. Madison. We won't breathe a word of it.

MADISON: (again, reluctantly) I think far more serious than the question of large and small states will be the issue of North versus South. The slavery question.

(General embarrassment.)

MASON: Mr. Madison, I'm glad you've said this. As a slave owner, I can tell you I am as opposed to it as any man. As you know, Mr. Jefferson and I have already persuaded the Virginia legislature to allow slave owners to give manumission to their slaves. Mr. Jefferson and I are both preparing to free our slaves upon our death.

PINCKNEY: Now, Colonel Mason, it may be easy enough for you to talk about freeing your slaves since Virginia is overstocked with slaves already. But in South Carolina, where the slaves' rate of death is much higher -

STERLING: Yes, well perhaps we shouldn't talk about this right now. General Pinckney, do you think I could interest you in a walk in the garden? It's such a beautiful evening, isn't it? (They depart.)

RITTENHOUSE: Yes, Colonel Mason, could you come with me a moment? There's someone I wanted you to meet. (They depart.)

MORRIS: Well, Mr. Madison, that was a lively subject you picked for us.

MADISON: I apologize.

WILSON: Oh, don't worry. It will blow up sooner or later.

MORRIS: The cache of gunpowder lying beneath the convention.

WILSON: Ay, beneath the whole country. By the way, Mr. Madison, which side will you be taking when this tormented issue finally arises?

(Madison is again extremely embarrassed.)

MORRIS: Oh come now, Mr. Wilson. Don't ask a Virginia man to tell you where he stands on slavery.

MADISON: Gentlemen, you are trifling with a very difficult subject.

MORRIS: Mr. Madison, no one is more opposed to slavery than I. I just don't enjoy humoring the pompous proclamations of these slave-holding republicans and their post-mortem declarations of independence.

MADISON: You must include both General Washington and myself in that company, Mr. Morris.

MORRIS: I realize that, Mr. Madison.

WILSON: Yes, Gouverneur, is there any of us really entitled to cast the first stone? I suspect if your holdings were in South Carolina rather than the Hudson Valley you'd probably be making a pretty good case for slavery yourself.

MORRIS: Never, Mr. Wilson. Never.

WILSON: Remember what our good friend Colonel Hamilton tells us about self-interest.

MORRIS: Yes, by the way, where is our friend Colonel Hamilton this evening?

MADISON: He is preparing a speech for the convention for tomorrow. He has decided to break his silence.

MORRIS: You mean we're finally going to hear a declaration for monarchy?

WILSON: An *elected* monarch, Gouverneur. The republican variety.

MORRIS: Splendid! I can't think of anything to enliven this stale convention better than a speech from Colonel Hamilton.

Act II, Scene 6

Independence Hall, June 18, 1787.

HAMILTON stands alone before the Convention.

HAMILTON: Mr.. Chairman, the honorable Dr. Franklin, distinguished members of this convention. I have hitherto been relatively silent out of respect for the superior age, abilities, and experience of the other delegates. However, I find the situation too serious to let any further scruples prevail. I am obliged to declare myself unfriendly to the plans of both Governor Randolph and Mr. Patterson.

Mr. Chairman, we must admit the state governments hold the loyalty of the people. They are familiar, honored, and respected. Moreover, those wielding power in them are reluctant to part with their prerogatives.

For that reason, I believe we must create a national government that is attractive and compelling enough to lift the loyalties of the people. What kind of system can fulfill that purpose? Here is what I propose:

Article I. The Supreme Legislative Power of the United States of American should be vested in two different bodies, the one being the Assembly, the other the Senate. The Assembly should be elected for three years, the Senate for life.

Article II. The Supreme Executive of the United States shall be vested in a single individual who shall serve for life or good behavior. The Electors for this office shall be chosen by the people. This executive shall have power to veto all laws passed by the legislature; direct all efforts in war and peace; make all treaties with the advice and consent of the Senate; and appoint the chief officers of Finance, War, and Foreign Affairs.

Article III. The judicial power shall be vested in a single system of federal courts, which shall have supreme authority to interpret any law the Congress and the executive may make.

Article IV. No state shall maintain its own armed forces or its own money. In all matters of difference between the states and the national government, the national government shall prevail. All laws passed by the states contrary to the Constitution shall be utterly void.

Will this be republican government? Yes, if the Senators and the Executive are elected by the people. Will some call it monarchy? Indeed they may. But it is a monarchy that is elected and therefore wholly acceptable and different.

Gentlemen, that is my proposal. I am aware this goes far beyond the ideas of most of the members present, yet I see no other recourse. The Union is disintegrating - perhaps already dissolved. We have no choice. For all these reasons, I beg you to consider the merits of my proposal.

(Meeting quickly breaks up. GOUVERNEUR MORRIS, MADISON, and WILSON approach Hamilton.)

MORRIS: Colonel Hamilton, that was magnificent. You've finally breathed some life into this convention.

HAMILTON: At the price of losing my seat, I'm afraid. The other New York delegates are about to leave, aren't they?

MADISON: I heard they had.

HAMILTON: Then I am a man without a country, Jemmy. I will probably leave as well. I'm afraid I have offended the majority.

MORRIS: Nonsense, Colonel Hamilton, you've won the respect of every delegate.

WILSON: Yes, why don't you join us at the reception?

HAMILTON: My mind is weary of receptions, Mr. Wilson.

MORRIS: I have a much better idea. I know a wonderful little tavern nearby. Let us repair there and obliterate all thought of senates and assemblies with strong drink.

WILSON: Capital, Gouverneur. Will you join us Colonel Hamilton?

HAMILTON: I suppose I will.

WILSON: You too, Mr. Madison?

MADISON: Very well, I'll come.

MORRIS: No one needs a sojourn in the field of Elysium more than our friend Mr. Madison.

WILSON: Well then, lead on, Gouverneur.

HAMILTON: *Lay* on, Gouverneur.

MADISON: "Lay on, Mac Duff!"

ALL: "And damned be him that first cries, `Hold, enough!'"

(They exit merrily.)

Act II, Scene 7

The City Tavern

MRS. HOUSE, COOT, NILES, ABRAHAM, and a young reporter, JARED PHILLIPS, sit around.   MADISON, HAMILTON, MORRIS, AND WILSON enter.

MORRIS: There you are, gentlemen, much more refined than our barbaric drawing rooms, wouldn't you say?

HAMILTON: Haven't we been here before?

MADISON: It was the first night.

HAMILTON: Yes, that's right.

MRS. HOUSE: Mr. Madison, Colonel Hamilton - oh, Mr. Morris, nice to see you again.

WILSON: You are well known among the innkeepers of Philadelphia, gentlemen.

MORRIS: We are men of the people, Mr. Wilson.

MRS. HOUSE: Make yourselves at home. What can I get for you fine, patriotic gentlemen?

HAMILTON: I'll have rum.

MADISON: Ale.

WILSON: Ale.

MORRIS: Rum.

MRS. HOUSE: I'll be with you in a moment. (She leaves.)

MORRIS: So, gentlemen, your fame has extended to the very barkeeps of Philadelphia.

MADISON: Alex and I stumbled in here one evening back in May.

MORRIS: No need for excuses, Mr. Madison. I'm sure your reputation as a scholar won't be despoiled by an occasional Bacchanalian revelry. (All laugh.)

(Coot, sitting at the bar, has caught Hamilton's eye. They exchange salutes.)

COOT: Evenin' Colonel Hamilton.

HAMILTON: Evening.

MORRIS: An old soldier, Colonel Hamilton?

HAMILTON: A patriot, Gouverneur.

WILSON: You're really much more a man of the people than you care to admit, aren't you Colonel?

HAMILTON: And much less than I would want the people to know.

MORRIS: Oh, don't be modest, Colonel.

HAMILTON: The people, my friend, are a great beast.

MORRIS: Well, we won't tell anyone you said that.

HOUSE: (returning). There we are, gentlemen. Ale, ale, and rum for Colonel Hamilton and Mr. Morris. Now stay as long as you like. I won't let anyone bother you.

(As she departs, Phillips comes over and asks her something. She admonishes him and indicates he should stay away from them.)

MORRIS: Gentlemen, here's to our country. Long may she stand.

HAMILTON: To the memory of thirteen petty, squabbling principalities. Long may they be forgotten.

ALL: Hear! Hear! (They toast.)

WILSON: Well, here we are in the middle of June and we don't have a senate, an assembly, a judiciary, or an executive.

MORRIS: On the contrary, Mr. Wilson, we have three assemblies, two judiciaries, five executives, and every delegate's personal conception idea of the Senate.

MADISON: Actually, we have Montesquieu's tripartite balance: Mr. Randolph's plan, Mr. Patterson's plan, and Alex's - all perfectly independent.

WILSON: Maybe we should just have three governments. That would be checks and balances, wouldn't it?

MORRIS: You've heard this rumor of dividing into three republics, I presume? New England, the Middle States, and the South?

HAMILTON: No, it won't happen that way. We will divide in two parts, North and South, with slavery the issue. Pennsylvania will be our battleground. We will water it with our blood every ten years.

(There is a moment of glum silence.)

WILSON: A rather depressing prospect, isn't it? (All murmur in assent.) What are we doing wrong?

HAMILTON: It's quite simple. Americans want a national government but they don't want to give it power to carry out its will.

WILSON: We don't trust ourselves.

MORRIS: I think it's the experience with Britain. We imagine every executive to be King George.

WILSON: Mr. Madison, what do you think?

MADISON: I agree with Gouverneur and Alex, but it's a bit more complex. We worry about executive tyrannies and aristocratic tyrannies, but we forget that the greatest tyranny of all is the tyranny of the majority.

WILSON and MORRIS: Well said. True.

MADISON: If men were angels, government wouldn't be necessary. Given human nature, though, what we need is some power to protect men from themselves. The popular impression is that we are here to devise a system for popular government. But the truth is, while republican government gives the *appearance* of popular rule, our real task is to create a government that can prevent the majority from overrunning itself and becoming a popular tyranny. We must create a government strong enough to carry out its will yet divided and weak enough so that it can restrain itself.

WILSON: (After absorbing this.) It couldn't be said any better, could it Mr. Morris?

HAMILTON: If we ever have a Constitution, it will be because of Jemmy.

WILSON: A toast to Mr. Madison.

MORRIS, HAMILTON, and WILSON: Hear! Hear!

MORRIS: Do you think Franklin understands all this?

HAMILTON: Franklin is senile.

MORRIS: Shame on you, Colonel Hamilton.

WILSON: I wouldn't go that far. He's a little forgetful at times and he tires easily. I mean after all, the man is 81 years old.

HAMILTON: I take it back. Dr. Franklin is not senile. His real problem is his rustic simplicity. He thinks the whole country can live like homely Quakers.

MORRIS: Franklin is often not as sophisticated as you would think.

MADISON: At least he didn't wear his coonskin cap.

HAMILTON: He is sophisticated enough to play the rustic in Paris and the sage in Philadelphia.

WILSON: Which is no small thing. The thing to realize about Franklin is that winning wars and charming Paris are only a diversion for him. He'd really rather be tinkering in his laboratory.

MORRIS: How do you think Washington would fare in Paris?

HAMILTON: The same as anywhere. He would be an immortal.

MORRIS: Oh, I don't know. There's a certain pose about it, don't you think?

WILSON: All majesty is pose. Do you think the King of England looks any different than you or I in his nightshirt?

MORRIS: (slapping his wooden leg) At least he has two legs!

MADISON: Or so we presume.

HAMILTON: No, with Washington it's more than pose. The man has prowess. Have you ever seen his hands?

WILSON: Immense.

HAMILTON: Twice the size of any other man's. Have you ever tried to keep up with him on horseback?

WILSON: He's the best rider in the country.

HAMILTON: Let me tell you a story. One day at Mount Vernon a couple of artists had come down to paint the General's portrait. After awhile they joined some servants in a game of throwing the hammer. They were out there with shirts off, sweating and straining, when the General happens by. "Having a go at the hammer?" he says. "Here, let me give it a try." Then he picks it up and with no more than a flick of his wrist hurls it far, far out, almost twice as far as anyone else had thrown it. "If any of you gentlemen start coming close," says the General, "give me a call and I'll try again."

(A moment of appreciation.)

WILSON: With Washington, all the legends are true.

MORRIS: Still, I find him very approachable, don't you?

WILSON: What do you mean, Gouverneur?

MORRIS: Oh, every time I see him standing in one of those reception lines, I want to go clap him on the shoulder and say, "My, General, it certainly is good to see you looking so well tonight."

WILSON: I don't think the General would appreciate that, Mr. Morris.

HAMILTON: Why don't you try?

MORRIS: Well, indeed I may.

MADISON: Alex feels he knows Washington's mind as well as you do, Gouverneur.

HAMILTON: I'll tell you what, Mr. Morris. I'll wager you a steak dinner and a bottle of wine at any restaurant in Philadelphia that you won't do as you just said - clap the General on the shoulder one evening and tell him he's looking well.

MORRIS: You have yourself a wager.

MADISON: Careful Gouverneur, the General might not appreciate this.

MORRIS: Nonsense, we've been friends for years.

(Coot has approached the table.)

COOT: Excuse me, Colonel Hamilton, I didn't mean to bother ye. I jes' wanted to tell ye not to fergit about our freedom.

HAMILTON: We haven't forgotten, sir.

COOT: That's what we fought for, y'know.

HAMILTON: I know, sir.

MORRIS: Colonel Hamilton wouldn't take anyone's freedom away, would he? Except perhaps a few minor delegates from Maryland.

WILSON: Excuse me, sir, did I hear you say you fought in the Revolution?

COOT: I did.

WILSON: What was your enlistment?

COOT: I fought the whole war, sir, from Boston to Yorktown.

WILSON: Well, that's commendable. Here, sit down.

COOT: That's alright, sir.

WILSON: No, please do.

MORRIS: Always ready to accommodate an old soldier.

COOT: (sits). I didn't actually get to Yorktown, sir. I got nicked in the leg and couldn't march. I went to Staten Island instead. Y'see General Washington wanted the British to think we wuz goin' for New York. So a bunch of us went pokin' 'round Staten Island askin' for boats and stuff - so they'd think we wuz gon' t'cross the Hudson. Meanwhile he sneaked pretty near the whole damned army down to Yorktown and - pfffft! - we pinned 'em on the coast.

MORRIS: It was a brilliant maneuver.

HAMILTON: Took the entire army from New Jersey to Yorktown in two weeks.

WILSON: What do you think of General Washington - as a commander, I mean?

72

COOT: (shrugs) Best there is. Some of the officers are pretty stuck on themselves. But Washington, he'll look ye right in th'eye.

MORRIS: I hope you're not referring to our good friend Colonel Hamilton here.

COOT: I didn't meet Colonel Hamilton during the war.

MORRIS: Well I'm sure you'd remember.

WILSON: What was the worst part of the war for you?

MADISON: Getting shot at, of course.

COOT: No, worst part for me was never gettin' nothin' t'eat. I figger in six year I probably ate onst every three days.

WILSON: Good old Congress.

HAMILTON: We could never get the simplest things done.

MORRIS: Were you at Valley Forge?

COOT: I was, sir.

MORRIS: What was that like?

HAMILTON: You could have asked me.

MORRIS: I mean from his standpoint.

COOT: It was bad, sir. I'll tell ye somethin' though, Morristown was worse.

HAMILTON: He's right.

WILSON: What year was that, '77?

MADISON: '78, I believe.

MORRIS: Was there starvation?

COOT: There was everythin'. I seen a grown man gnaw his own foot off onst. Foot froze right up on him, hard as a rock. Man hadn't had anything to eat in two weeks. Gnawed his own foot right down to the bone. He died afterwards, I think.

(There is a long, respectful silence.)

WILSON: Was that the worst you ever saw?

COOT: There was probably worse than that. Ye fergit after awhile.

WILSON: What do you think of Congress?

COOT: Congress?

MORRIS: That illustrious body that convenes here occasionally in Philadelphia?

COOT: Ye mean this convention that's goin' on, sir?

MORRIS: No, we are a different group.

COOT: Y'mean the one Dr. Franklin sits on?

MORRIS: No, that is the Pennsylvania state legislature. I mean the one that is now meeting in New York.

COOT: Oh, ye mean the one the soldiers chased out a few years ago.

HAMILTON: A formidable reputation, eh, gentlemen?

MADISON: This is our national government.

MORRIS: Yes, what do you think of them - if you haven't told us already.

COOT: They all seem 'bout the same to me. I never pay much attention to 'em.

MORRIS: I'm sure that's best.

HAMILTON: Much more sensible than we are.

WILSON: What do you do for a living, my good man?

COOT: I'm a trapper. I been all the way up through the Wyoming territory, up into Michigan.

MADISON: You meet the Indian populations up there?

COOT: (Shrugs) I don't worry 'bout 'em too much, sir. They minds their own business, I looks after mine.

MORRIS: What do you think of slavery?

WILSON: Oh come now, Gouverneur, let's not tax the man.

MORRIS: This is the vox populi, Mr. Wilson. How can we form a government if we don't know what this man is thinking?

COOT: I think it's a bad thing, sir. I don't want to be anywhere near it.

(CICERO is walking by at this moment and Morris buttonholes him.)

MORRIS: Here, let's get it from the horse's mouth. Excuse me, young man, what do you think of slavery?

CICERO: Who, me?

HAMILTON: Gouverneur - !

MORRIS: Yes, we're sampling the vox populi. We'd like to know your opinion -

WILSON: Gouverneur, I must ask you to desist.

CICERO: I don't know no "vox pop-a-li," sir.

WILSON: Really, Gouverneur.

HAMILTON: Save your social graces for General Washington, Mr. Morris.

MORRIS: (To Cicero) Well, we'll let you go now but I'd like to ask you sometime. (Releases Cicero. Phillips has now approached the table.) Well, here's another member of the public. What can we do for you, sir?

MRS. HOUSE: (Rushing to intervene.) Now sir, I told you to leave these gentlemen alone.

MORRIS: That's alright, madam, we can defend ourselves. Here, let's have another round.

HAMILTON: (indicating Morris) He's had too many already.

MORRIS: Drinks all around. (To Phillips) There, young man, would you like to give us your opinion on state debts? What is your name anyway?

PHILLIPS: I'm Jared Phillips, journalist for the Philadelphia Gazette.

WILSON and HAMILTON: Oh, no! Good gracious!

MORRIS: Hoisted in our own petard!

PHILLIPS: You gentlemen are attending the convention?

MADISON: Our lips are sealed.

MORRIS: Young man, your instincts are superb. We are the very men who are trying to write you a Constitution. This is Dr. Franklin, this is General Washington, this is Thomas Jefferson, and I am General Lafayette.

WILSON: He's in high spirits.

MADISON: Drunk with Republican virtue.

MORRIS: (trying to introduce Coot) This is Mr. . . . . what did you say your name was, sir?

COOT: They call me "Coot."

MORRIS: Yes, this is Mr. Coot. He's our delegate from the Indian territory.

WILSON: Let's be clear, now. This is Colonel Alexander Hamilton, this is James Madison, I am James Wilson, and our genial host is Gouverneur Morris.

PHILLIPS: (scribbling, to Madison) What was your name again, sir?

MADISON: James Madison.

HAMILTON: You'll read it in the history books.

PHILLIPS: I was wondering if you gentlemen could comment on a few rumors that have been circulating the convention.

WILSON: Our lips are sealed.

HAMILTON: Well if they're rumors, they must be true.

MORRIS: Yes, what do you know? Tell us.

PHILLIPS: Well sir, it's been said that the delegates are conspiring together to deprive the people of their liberties.

MADISON, HAMILTON, WILSON: Oh no! Good grief! What nonsense!

MORRIS: Why yes! That's brilliant. How did you find out?

PHILLIPS: I have my sources.

MORRIS: Tell us everything you're heard

PHILLIPS: Well - let me remind you this is only a rumor - it's been said that some members of the convention wish to establish a monarchy.

WILSON, MADISON: This is absurd. Ridiculous.

MORRIS: Right again! This is marvelous.

HAMILTON: Have you heard the rumor of King George?

PHILLIPS: What?

MADISON: Alex, please.

HAMILTON: (whispering conspiratorially) KING GEORGE III! He's attending the Convention!

PHILLIPS: That's not true.

HAMILTON: Yes it is. Mr. Gerry of Massachusetts wants him crowned King of the Americas at a salary of four pounds seven shillings a year. Dr. Franklin wants him to work without compensation.

MADISON: He's joking.

HAMILTON: You're rival publication has the story.

PHILLIPS: Which one?

HAMILTON: The Baltimore something-or-other.

PHILLIPS: I can't believe you, sir.

WILSON: My dear fellow, although we admire your diligence, we really cannot talk to you. All the delegates are sworn to secrecy. We even have sentries posted at the windows to prevent eavesdropping.

PHILLIPS: I have a cousin who's a sentry.

WILSON, MADISON, and HAMILTON: Aha! So that's it!

PHILLIPS: (backtracking) He has told me nothing.

MORRIS: The counterfeit sentry unveiled.

HAMILTON: Mr. Chairman, I move that from now on all sentries be deafened cannoneers so they cannot eavesdrop on our deliberations.

MORRIS: What else have you learned of our conspiracies?

PHILLIPS: Well, gentlemen, let me remind you, this is only a rumor. But is it true that some delegates have suggested that George Washington wear a toga?

(General uproarious laughter all around.)

WILSON: This is too much.

MORRIS: My dear friend, you have restored my faith in the folly of mankind.

HAMILTON: Mr. Coot, are you listening to all this?

COOT: (says something inaudible.)

HAMILTON: I'm sorry, what did you say, sir?

COOT: I said it makes me glad I can't read.

(All laugh again.)

WILSON: Yes, you're much better off.

MORRIS: Young man, we are all going to wear togas - James, you'd look quite handsome in a toga - and we're going to dress the common people in animal skins. We'll call it *The Decline and Fall of the Roman Empire*. Have you read that book, gentlemen?

WILSON: I don't have time to read anything anymore, Mr. Morris.

HAMILTON: I confess I got through only half.

MADISON: I gave up around the reign of Diocletian.

MORRIS: Yes, Gibbon doth have the power to exhaust a man.

PHILLIPS: Do you think the American empire will survive, gentlemen?

(They are taken aback.)

HAMILTON: Empire?! You call this squabbling nest of petty principalities an empire?

PHILLIPS: We have a destiny, sir. Rome started with less territory.

MORRIS: (In mock amazement.) We should have this fellow address our convention.

PHILLIPS: I believe the county in which a man lives shapes his mind. The English have always been insular, despite their conquests. The French are hemmed in by their mountains. But we have a vast territory before us. Even the humblest man knows he has empire in his blood.

HAMILTON: Remarkable!

WILSON: Astonishing!

MORRIS: A philosopher!

MADISON: Yes, Tom Paine, I believe.

PHILLIPS: But –

MADISON: *Common Sense,* isn't it? It's in there somewhere.

PHILLIPS: Yes, but how did you –

WILSON: Mr. Madison here is very well read.

MADISON: Somewhere around the middle, isn't it?

MORRIS: So, another disciple of Tom Paine. And where is our illustrious scribbler these days?

PHILLIPS: He's in England, sir. I was hoping he would attend this convention.

(Another round of uproarious laughter.)

HAMILTON: Future generations will bless their creator that Tom Paine did not attend this convention.

PHILLIPS: What do you mean, sir?

WILSON: Tom Paine is the sort of fellow who's good at tearing down governments. We're in the business of building them up.

PHILLIPS: He speaks the truth, sir. He speaks for the people.

MORRIS: My good fellow, we all speak for the people. The people speak for the people. You newspapers wield far more power than we do. The only question is whether we, your humble servants, can keep the people from tearing each other apart and the country along with it.

PHILLIPS: You shouldn't criticize newspapers, sir. Thomas Jefferson says he'd rather have newspapers without government than government without newspapers.

WILSON: And we may have it much sooner than Mr. Jefferson ever expected.

HAMILTON: Future generations will bless their creator Mr. Jefferson was not at this convention, either.

MORRIS: But we have Mr. Mason, the great slaveholding republican to speak for him.

HAMILTON: A toast to Mr. Mason!

MORRIS and WILSON: Hear! Hear!

MADISON: Gentlemen, gentlemen, I must disagree. (Everyone quiets down.) I do not fear Mr. Jefferson's voice, nor Mr. Mason's voice, nor even Tom Paine's voice for that matter. I think our experience has shown that it is the moderation of each individual, rather than the brilliance of any one mind, that is leading us forward. The useless ideas are quickly discarded while the fruitful ones win acceptance no matter in whose brain they are born. I myself have found many of my preconceptions to be completely impractical.

(A moment of general embarrassment.)

WILSON: Mr. Madison here is a very tolerant fellow.

HAMILTON: The best man among us. Some day he will be known as the Father of this Constitution.

MORRIS: A toast to Mr. Madison!

ALL: Hear! Hear!

WILSON: Gentlemen, I must be going. We have another long day ahead listening to Mr. Luther Martin of Maryland.

HAMILTON: Is it Luther Martin or Martin Luther?

MORRIS: Yes, I make the same mistake.

HAMILTON: To Maryland on Delaware! (Toasts.)

MORRIS: To Delaware on Maryland! (Toasts again.)

(Mrs. House approaches.)

WILSON: Never mind, madam. I believe our little party is breaking up. (He begins to settle accounts with her.)

PHILLIPS: But gentlemen, you haven't answered my questions. Are you considering a monarchy?

MADISON: Young man - although I dare say you are not much younger than myself - I beg you to print only the truth. And the truth is that, although we have made some progress, we are still a long, long way from claiming any fruit to our deliberations.

PHILLIPS: That's not a very good story, sir.

MADISON: It may not be a good story, but it is the truth, and the truth is the only good story. Good night, sir.

MORRIS: Goodnight everyone.

ALL: Goodnight.

PHILLIPS: Good night, gentlemen. (Calling after them.) Thank you for your information.

Act II, Scene 8

George and Martha Washington's bedroom.

(GEORGE WASHINGTON sits on the edge of the bed. MARTHA still seems asleep.)

MARTHA: What's the matter, darling.

GEORGE: Nothing.

MARTHA: Can't sleep?

GEORGE: No.

MARTHA: Are you worried?

GEORGE: Yes.

MARTHA: About what?

GEORGE: The fate of my country.

MARTHA: I thought you said things were going well.

GEORGE: Not entirely.

MARTHA: Didn't you say there was hope?

GEORGE: There was for a while. Now we've bogged down.

MARTHA: Over what?

GEORGE: Oh, the big states versus the small states. The composition of the Senate. Everything.

MARTHA: Why don't you give a speech, dear? Tell them what you think.

GEORGE: I can't speak.

MARTHA: Certainly you can! You speak beautifully.

GEORGE: I mean I can't . . . . debate. My thoughts come too slowly. Five minutes after a point has been made, I think of exactly what I want to say. But by then it's too late.

MARTHA: Well write it down, dear. Your letters are always so beautiful.

GEORGE: I can't read my letters at a convention.

(There is a moment of silence.)

MARTHA: You worry too much, darling.

GEORGE: I cannot do otherwise.

MARTHA: You don't have to do everything, dear. You've already done so much. The country can go on without you for a while, can't it?

GEORGE: I look forward to it every day.

(Another silence.)

MARTHA: I'll tell you what, dear. You know that way you have of expressing disapproval, when you pull your chin back and stare down at someone? (She does an impersonation. He smiles a bit.) Well, every time a delegate says something you think is wrong, you just pull your chin back and give them that look. And you know that way you have of expressing approval, where your chin relaxes and your eyes smile? Well, every time someone says something you think is right, you give them that look. (She has him amused by now.) They'll understand. Every delegate will know exactly what you think about everything.

GEORGE: (now completely relaxed) You're a good woman, Martha.

MARTHA: Now come to bed.

✦

Act II, Scene 9

The Convention Floor, June 28, 1787.

LUTHER MARTIN, of Maryland, is addressing the floor. It is evident he has been speaking a long, long time. He mops his brow frequently. There are few delegates present and they sit uncomfortably or wander aimlessly. Downstage, HAMILTON and MORRIS confer as Martin carries on in the background.

MARTIN: And so I say to the delegates once again, as John Locke has said, when these states threw off the yoke of Britain they were placed in a perfect state of nature. As Mr. Locke has described it, this state of nature is one in which each individual remains entitled to certain inalienable rights, including those of life, liberty, and property. Let me read a minute from Mr. Locke:

"To understand Political Power right, and derive it from its Original, we must consider what State all Men are naturally in, and that is, a State of Perfect Freedom to offer their Actions, and dispose of their Possessions, and Persons as they think fit."

Now the most important possession of each individual in a State of Nature is the right to equal representation in any legislative body that represents the whole. A state cannot surrender this right without violating its own person, just as an individual cannot surrender his right without violating his own person, as Mr. Locke has written.

HAMILTON: How long has it been?

MORRIS: Three days.

HAMILTON: How long can he go on?

MORRIS: Probably three months.

HAMILTON: (Listening again.) How many times can a man say the same thing without dulling his own brain?

MORRIS: It's easy when you have but one thing to say.

(MADISON approaches.)

HAMILTON: Seeking shelter from the storm, Jemmy? (Madison shrugs.)

MORRIS: You're not keeping your journal, Mr. Madison. How will posterity know what Mr. Martin had to say?

MADISON: I've gotten the gist of it.

MORRIS: I hope you're writing down my illustrious remarks, Mr. Madison. I want future generations to remember what I said.

MADISON: It's all in there, Gouverneur.

(At that moment, Martin falters. He takes a seat.)

MARTIN: Mr. Chairman, if I may beg your leave, I think I must stop and rest a moment.

MORRIS: The ship of state reels.

HAMILTON: The Maryland typhoon has blown itself out.

WILSON: Have you seen this newspaper, Colonel Hamilton?

GORHAM: (rapping for order). Will the delegates please resume their seats or face quorum call?

HAMILTON: (reads): "A certain military man who distinguished himself during the Revolution and now plays a prominent role at the current convention has suggested that a monarchy was not out of the realm of possibility for the new government of the United States." (Incredulous.) This is scandal!

MORRIS: Let me see that.

WILSON: It gets better.

MARTIN: (resumes his place. As he speaks, Hamilton, Wilson, and Morris talk over.) And so, Mr. Chairman, let me say once again in conclusion, the small states retain their inherent Natural right, as Mr. Locke has described it, to an equal vote in Congress. They cannot surrender this right without violating their own liberty. Mr. Chairman, we cannot join any union in which we must surrender our natural rights. It is against nature. We must have an equal vote in Congress. Without this we will not consolidate. That is all I have to say.

MORRIS: (reading): "This delegate also hinted that the intervention of a well-known foreign monarch into the proceedings of the convention was not altogether impossible. These revelations were made under the most confidential conditions at an informal meeting place very near the State House." This is libel.

WILSON: That's how journals are made, Gouverneur.

GORHAM: (As Martin finishes, he raps loudly.) Would the delegates please resume their seats for a discussion on the representation in Congress? (The delegates scurry back to their seats.) The chair recognizes Mr. Baldwin.

BALDWIN: Mr. Chairman, although Mr. Martin has made his case here at great length – great length - let me contribute by saying that as a delegate from Georgia, I still believe that the states must make some sacrifice. Though from a small state, I consider myself a citizen of the United States.

GERRY: Mr. Chairman, in contradiction to what Mr. Martin has said, I don't believe the states were ever independent states. The advocates of the states have become intoxicated with this idea of their own sovereignty. It is for this reason the Confederacy is dissolving and we find ourselves adrift. I beg that we resolve this issue for the fate of the union depends on it. If we don't act, I doubt if Congress will meet again.

MADISON: Mr. Chairman, in framing a system we wish to last for ages, let us now lose sight of the changes the ages will bring. Isn't it likely that the large territories to the West will one day be populated and may overshadow the former colonies? The distinction between small and large states will eventually fade with the growth of the union.

HAMILTON: Mr. Chairman, let me observe several circumstances. The three largest states are separated not only by distance but by interest. The business of Massachusetts is seafaring, of Pennsylvania wheat, of Virginia tobacco. Isn't it more likely that they will form alliances with nearby states than collaborate with other strictly because of size?

MARTIN: I can agree, Mr. Chairman, but I still do not see the need for two houses of Congress. The present system remains adequate. The contempt we see for Congress is really a contempt for national government in general.

WILSON: Mr. Chairman, I have done a small calculation here and found that those delegates who remain affixed to the idea of equal representation for every state constitute less than one-fourth of the country's population. The question before us is this.

Shall such a small minority of the population frustrate the union of an entire country? Does every state wish to become its own Rhode Island?

SHERMAN: Mr. Chairman, the objection of Mr. Wilson that the minority will rule the majority is simply not true. Rather it is the few that must fear being oppressed by the many. Although scoffed at, this possibility of the large states combining is not imaginary. Say there was a commercial treaty in which three or four free ports were to be established. Is it not likely that the three states would combine so that Boston, Philadelphia, and Norfolk were chosen? I cannot for all my efforts see the need for two houses in Congress. If it must be done, however, let us say the states shall be representation by population in one and by equal representation in the other.

WILSON: Mr. Chairman, although I respect the close reasonings of Mr. Sherman, it seems to me that Connecticut is the least likely candidate to be defending the current Congress. That state has passed a law positively refusing to collect taxes for the national government.

SHERMAN: Let me assure Mr. Wilson that whatever shortcomings may exist, Connecticut is entirely federal. We had more troops in the field throughout the war than Virginia.

DAVIE: Can someone enlighten me on one point? The Senate, as I understand, is to be a small, select council intended to preserve us from the democratic excesses of the Assembly. Yet if it is to have representation by population, then one vote for Georgia must be equaled by several dozen from Virginia. If this is so, then how are we to prevent the Senate from growing just as large and unwieldy as the Assembly?

WILSON: I admit the point is an embarrassment. If the smallest states are to have even one representative, the largest must have

40 or 50. In order to avoid this, I would consent to a compromise where the ratio is no more than four-or-five-to-one.

ELLSWORTH: I would like to reiterate the suggestion just made by my colleague Mr. Sherman a moment ago, that the states should be represented by population in one house and by an equal number of delegates in the other. It seems to me this is sufficient grounds for compromise. I am not a halfway man, yet I prefer doing half of what is good than nothing at all.

KING: Mr. Chairman, it is obvious that the small states remain fixed and unalterable in their opposition. If we accept this argument, then we are simply creating the same Congress we have now, which has been an utter failure. I must tell you, my feelings for my country are more harrowed than I can express. I fear this is our last opportunity for establishing our liberty before we cut ourselves asunder. I cannot therefore but repeat my amazement that when a just government founded on representation of the *people* is so close at hand, we should founder on this idea of preserving the artificial and illusory importance of *states*.

BEDFORD: Gentlemen, I must express my skepticism in the assurance of our opponents that the large states will not abuse their dominating influence. Look at this convention. Are we not all expressing our own self-interest? Georgia is a small state but votes with the large because she expects to be large one day. South Carolina votes with the small because her territory is already hemmed in. And so on up the entire seaboard. Given the opportunity in any forum, will not each state act in its own self-interest?

We have been told with a dictatorial air that this is the last moment for achieving good government, yet I am under no such apprehensions. If the large states see fit to dissolve the Confederation, the small ones will find some foreign ally of more honor and good faith to take them by the hand and do them justice.

ELLSWORTH: Mr. Chairman, I am willing to participate in a national government, but where I look for the preservation of my rights, I turn to the state government. My happiness depends on their existence as much as a newborn infant depends on its mother's milk. I am sorry to express myself this way, but I can find no other.

KING: Mr. Chairman, I am for preserving the states for the purposes suggested by Mr. Ellsworth. I cannot let pass, however, the language of the honorable gentleman from Delaware who has just declared himself ready to turn for protection to some foreign hand. I am grieved that such a thought could enter his heart. For myself, I would never turn to a foreign power.

PINCKNEY: Mr. Chairman, I cannot express my alarms for the consequences for our country if we do not reach an agreement here. I consider this convention the last appeal to regular experiment. Congress has failed in every effort to amend the Federal system and nothing has prevented the dissolution of the union except this convention itself. Since we are almost exactly divided, let us appoint a committee to try to reach a compromise.

MARTIN: I will consent to a committee, but I must repeat the smaller states will not join any compromise that diminishes their sovereignty.

G. MORRIS: I agree that we are about equally divided and should appoint a committee. But let this in no way suggest that the large states will accede to the unreasonable demands of the smaller ones.

Make no mistake, gentlemen, this country must be united. If persuasion does not unite us, the sword will. I came here as a representative of America and I flatter myself also that I came representing to some degree the whole human race. For the whole human race will be affected by the proceedings of the convention. I wish, then, that we would extend our views beyond this moment in time, beyond the narrow limits of our political origin, and think instead of the ages and ages that lie before us.

SHERMAN: Gentlemen, we are at a full stop. Since there does not seem to be any resolution to our differences, let us appoint a committee to see if it can hit upon some expedient.

BEDFORD: Mr. Chairman, I find what I have said about the small states being taken by the hand has been misunderstood. I did not mean to imply that these states would court some foreign power but only that if the union should dissolve some foreign nation might find it expedient to take the smaller states by the hand. For this I apologize.

But is there not also an apology due in what Mr. Morris has just said about uniting this country by the sword? To hear such language without response would be to renounce my feelings as a man and my duties as a citizen.

GERRY: Gentlemen, gentlemen, something must be done. We are not only disappointing America here, we are disappointing the whole world. Consider the state we will be thrown into by a failure of our Union. We shall have no umpire to settle our disputes and will be left to the mercy of events. There must be concessions on both sides. Let us form a committee out of a member from each state and try to find a resolution.

WILSON: I am sorry Mr. Chairman but I must object on obvious grounds. While purporting to resolve the issue, such a committee will be making its decision on the very basis we are opposing - one vote for every state. We must find some better form of representation before even this issue can be considered.

FRANKLIN: Mr. Chairman, my I say a word here? (Rises.)

The small progress we have made after eight or nine weeks of continual reasonings is methinks a melancholy proof of the imperfections of Human Understanding. We have gone back to ancient history and viewed modern Europe in searching for models of republican government, yet find none of these suitable to our needs.

In the situation of this assembly, groping in the dark, as it were, in search of political truth, how is it, Sir, that we have not once thought of humbly addressing ourselves to the Father of Lights?

In the beginning of the contest with Great Britain, when all were sensible of the dangers we were entering, we held daily prayer in this room. Our prayers, Sir, were heard and graciously answered. All of us who were engaged in that struggle observed frequent instances of a superintending Providence in our favor. It is to that kind Providence that we owe this opportunity of consulting in peace with one another over the future of our nation.

And have we now forgotten that powerful Friend? I have lived a long time, Sir, and the longer I live, the more I am convinced of this truth - that *God governs in the affairs of men!* And if a sparrow cannot fall to the ground without His notice, is it probable that an empire can rise without his guidance?

I therefore beg leave to move that henceforth prayers be offered in this Assembly each morning imploring the assistance of Heaven and its blessings on our deliberations, and that one or more of the clergy of this city be requested to officiate in that service.

SHERMAN: Seconded.

HAMILTON: Mr. Chairman, I must express some apprehension about this idea. However proper it may have been at the beginning of our deliberations, it might now lead the public to believe the Convention has become mired in dissention.

SHERMAN: It is just the opposite. If our dissentions become plain and we show no efforts to heal them, the effects will be much worse.

WILLIAMSON: Mr. Chairman, may I make a small point. The reason a clergyman has not been hired to date is simple. The Convention has no funds for it.

RANDOLPH: Mr. Chairman, since we are approaching the Fourth of July holiday, may I make two proposals. First, that a sermon be preached in this room on the anniversary of our glorious Declaration of Independence. Second, that we take advantage of the recess to appoint a committee of one member from each state to meet over the holiday and try to find some resolution to our differences. The members I would suggest are: Mr. Gerry, of Massachusetts; Mr. Ellsworth, of Connecticut; Mr. Yates, of New York; Mr. Patterson, of New Jersey; Dr. Franklin, of Pennsylvania; Mr. Bedford, of Delaware; Mr. Martin, of Maryland; Mr. Mason, of Virginia; Mr. Davie, of North Carolina; Mr. Rutledge, of South Carolina; and Mr. Baldwin, of Georgia.

FRANKLIN: Seconded.

GORHAM: All in favor?

ALL: Aye.

GORHAM: Very well, we will adjourn for two days in honor of the Fourth of July. Please make plans to attend the sermon that will be preached in this room on our national holiday.

Act III, Scene 1

City Tavern, September 1, 1787.

MADISON, MRS. HOUSE, MR. WHATELY, and NILES are present. CICERO is in and out, cleaning tables.

HOUSE: Such a lovely day, Mr. Madison. You should be out enjoying yourself.

WHATELY: Still a bit hot, isn't it?

HOUSE: Oh, nonsense, Mr. Whately. Always complaining. You should be outside too, not sitting here drinking your life away.

WHATELY: Madam, I am not drinking my life away. I am collecting my thoughts.

NILES: He must have a pretty good collection by now.

WHATELY: Madam, are you saying you would prosper more if I were not constantly –

HOUSE: Look at George Washington. You don't see him sitting —

NILES: Hey, you know who I seed riding down the street yesterday? George Washington himself! On a beautiful gray horse. Going out to the old campground at Valley Forge. Boy what a time we had out there that winter. Lost my big toe. Froze right up on me, see? It ain't so easy to walk without a big toe, y'know.

WHATELY: I am sorry to hear that, sir.

NILES: Say Mr. Madison, you think when you're' finished with this here convention, think you could see about getting me some kinda pension or somethin' on account of this big toe?

HOUSE: Will you leave Mr. Madison alone, sir? He's got more to worry about than your big toe.

MADISON: That's alright, madam. Empires have fallen over less.

NILES: See, what'd I tell you?

WHATELY: Mr. Madison, sir, I know you're bound by your oath of secrecy. But I'm a man who likes to concern himself with the public business. And I was wondering -

HOUSE: Mr. Whately, don't even ask -

WHATELY: (Ignoring her.) Does the situation look favorable for our country?

HOUSE: Mr. Whately . . . .

MADISON: It's alright, madam. I think I can speak generally. Sir, our deliberations have taken much longer than we expected, but I believe there is now reason for optimism.

WHATELY: Excellent! Mr. Madison, I hope you appreciate how indebted we are for what you've all done this summer, deliberating in the midst of these torrid, tropical conditions.

HOUSE: Must be terrible, all stuffed up in that little room.

MADISON: It's been bearable.

WHATELY: Mr. Madison. I wonder what are the grounds for your optimism?

HOUSE: Mr. Whately, you are being unpatriotic.

MADISON: Sir, I don't think I would be breaking my oath to say that we ran into one great impediment at a certain point, but it now appears we have overcome that difficulty.

WHATELY: Wonderful. And could I enquire of the manner in which it was resolved?

MADISON: It was a compromise.

WHATELY: A compromise! Isn't that wonderful. You know, Mr. Madison, I am a great believer in compromise.

NILES: Why don't you go in there and show 'em how it's done, eh? Why'n't you show George Washington how it's done?

HOUSE: (whispering) Just ignore him, gentlemen.

WHATELY: Mr. Madison, and may I inquire, was this a compromise that was reached just after the Fourth of July?

HOUSE: Mr. Whately! I'm appalled.

MADISON: (Taken back a little.) You seem to have very good information, sir.

WHATELY: Just my observation of the general demeanor of the delegates.

MADISON: That's very perceptive of you, sir. Yes, there was a general compromise reached at about that time. Since then everything's been a bit easier. We're just taking off a few days to collect out thoughts.

HOUSE: Who was it thought of the compromise, - if you don't mind my askin', Mr. Madison?

MADISON: No one in particular. We appointed a committee and they came back with a suggestion that found approval.

HOUSE: I'll bet it was Dr. Franklin, wasn't it? He's such a clever man.

MADISON: Dr. Franklin was on the committee. But I think it was Mr. Sherman of Connecticut who first suggested the idea.

NILES: Where is Connecticut anyhow? Up around New York somewheres?

HOUSE: (whispers) Don't bother with him, gentlemen.

MADISON: It lies between New York and Massachusetts.

NILES: I been to New York but I never been to Connecticut.

HOUSE: Kind of a dull town, isn't it, that New York? Nothing half as exciting as Philadelphia.

MADISON: It has its virtues, madam.

WHATELY: So it was Mr. Sherman who resolved the crisis.

NILES: Never want to, neither.

MADISON: There were many minds at work on it, sir.

HOUSE: Is he as clever as Dr. Franklin, this Mr. Sherman?

MADISON: I don't think so, madam. But it matters not. The genius of this convention has not been the brilliance of any one mind but the willingness of so many to be led where they never expected to go.

WHATELY: That's very well said, Mr. Madison.

MADISON: It is also true.

HOUSE: So what kind of government are you going to give us, Mr. Madison, if you don't mind my askin'. It won't be a king, will it? The people don't want a king.

MADISON: I can't say for sure now but we hope it will be something acceptable to the people.

NILES: It better be.

HOUSE: Don't be impolite, sir.

NILES: The people rule this country, you know.

MADISON: I can assure you, sir, we are very well aware of that.

WHATELY: So pardon my asking, Mr. Madison, but are there any other impediments remaining?

MADISON: Well there is one other issue. I'm not sure we can resolve it. We may have to work around it.

WHATELY: And may I hazard a guess as to what it might be, sir?

MADISON: You may try, I suppose.

WHATELY: Slavery.

MADISON: (A little taken back again.) Well, once again you are quite perceptive, sir.

WHATELY: Mr. Madison, this slavery business is an abomination, a pall on our country. I abhor it with all my being. But do you know, Mr. Madison, I have a wonderful idea for resolving this issue. Even now I am putting aside a small amount of money in support of it. I believe we must return our black brethren to shores of Africa, reuniting them with the homeland from whence we wrenched them lo these many, many decades ago. Otherwise, I must agree with our beloved Thomas Jefferson when he says he fears for the future of our country because of slavery. By the way, Mr. Madison, did you now I once met Mr. Jefferson right on the steps of the House of Burgesses?

HOUSE: Mr. Whately, you are not going to tell that story again. I have heard that story so many times -

WHATELY: But our guest has not, madam. Have you ever met Mr. Jefferson, Mr. Madison?

MADISON: I had a letter from him just this morning.

WHATELY: (Taken back himself.) Oh. Well, then you know whereof I speak. Now the time I met Mr. Jefferson -

HOUSE: Mr. Whately. .

WHATELY: Madam, you hear the same stories told over and over in this establishment.

HOUSE: I do not, sir. I never allow a story to be told more than once beneath this roof. If ever I hear the same story . . .

(There is a long moment of embarrassment.)

Ah, Mr. Madison. There's something I've been meaning to tell you. Do you remember that night you can in here last spring, when it was raining so bad?

MADISON: I do.

HOUSE: And you remember that story you told about the man and the hat and the mud?

103

MADISON: You'd heard it before.

HOUSE: Mr. Whately himself had told it just a few moments before.

MADISON: I realized that almost immediately, madam. But I thank you for your indulgence at my stale efforts of humor. It was but a foreshadowing of the tolerance and courtesy we have all been willing to extend to each other at this convention.

As for your plans for the repatriation of slaves, sir, I do not believe it can accomplish much. I am a Virginian myself and if you could see the rapid rise in the slave population you would realize the notion is quite impractical. The slaves have been with us 150 years. They are as native as we are. I doubt if the majority would accept repatriation anyway, even it were offered.

WHATELY: Yes, but they would be free men, Mr. Madison! Doesn't that mean something? Oh, look, where's the boy? Cicero, come here a minute?

CICERO: (Re-entering.) Yessuh.

WHATELY: Cicero, come here. I'm going to ask you a question. Do you mind?

CICERO: No suh.

WHATELY: Cicero, if offered the chance, wouldn't you prefer to return to your native Africa?

CICERO: No, suh. I lives here in Philadelphia.

WHATELY: But I mean, wouldn't you like to return to your native homeland a free man?

CICERO: I's free here, suh. We's all free here in Philadelphia.

WHATELY: But if you were a slave in Virginia or South Carolina, wouldn't you dream of returning to Africa rather than being held in bondage?

CICERO: I was neva' no slave, suh. My momma and daddy ran away. That's how we got to Philadelphia.

WHATLEY: But your native homeland! The beloved continent of Africa! (Slightly exasperated.)

MADISON: Cicero, do you think you could learn to read?

CICERO: I reads, suh. I reads real good. My daddy taught me.

WHATELY: Well I don't know . . . .

CICERO: I show you, suh. I reads it right out of the Bible.

WHATELY: Well I doubt if you'll find a Bible in this establishment.

(Mrs. House wordlessly produces a Bible from beneath the counter. Niles is conspicuously ignoring all this.)

CICERO: That's right, I read it right out of old Leviticus. (Flips pages, then reads slowly):

"Or if he should touch the un-clean-ness of man, what-so-ever un-clean-ness it be; when he knoweth of it, then he shall be `gwilty.'
"And when he shall be `gwilty' in one of these things, he shall confess that he hath sinned and shall bring his trespass offering unto the Lord."

MADISON: (after a long moment of silence) Cicero, the word is "guilty."

CICERO: "G-u-i-l-t-y." That be "guilty?"

MADISON: The "u" is silent.

CICERO: I know that word. Sure I know that word! That be like when you hurt somebody and you be feelin' bad about it, ain't that right? That's "guilty," ain't it?

MADISON: That's correct, Cicero.

CICERO: Sure I know that word! Cause I be readin' it all this time, you see, but I didn't reco'nize it. But I knows it. Sure I know that word! That be "guilty."

MADISON: That's right, Cicero. And one day a long, long time from now, when things are very different in this country, I believe my countrymen will feel very, very guilty about what we have done to your people.

CICERO: Dat's true, suh.

MADISON: It may be a long, long time.

WHATELY: Can you forgive us, sir?

CICERO: God fo'give you, suh. My people be free some day. He fo'give you.

MADISON: Yes, but will we ever be able to forgive ourselves. Good people, I must be going. I have much work to do. But I thank you for your kindness. The hospitality you have shown us here in Philadelphia has been as integral to our success as anything that has occurred within our chambers.

HOUSE: That's very kind of you, sir.

ALL: Good-bye, Mr. Madison. Good day. (He leaves.)

HOUSE: What a wonderful young man.

CICERO: Very nice man. Very nice.

HOUSE: I don't think he could be more than thirty, could he?

WHATELY: Much too young for your fancies, madam.

HOUSE: Mr. Whately! I do not believe you said that!

WHATELY: (Expansive.) Good people, we are witnessing extraordinary events in Philadelphia this summer. Historic events. We are founding a country.

NILES: George Washington's the father of his country.

HOUSE: They're all our fathers. Even little Mr. Madison. They're our patriotic fathers.

WHATELY: They are our *founders*, madam. They are founding a nation.

HOUSE: They're our *fathers*, Mr. Whately. They are -

(A moment of recognition. They clink glasses.)

TOGETHER: Our Founding Fathers!

Act III, Scene 2

Independence Hall, September 5, 1787.

WASHINGTON again presides.

G. MORRIS: Mr. Chairman, on the question of representation in the Assembly, I move to insert the word "free" before the word "inhabitants." Upon what principle is it that slaves shall be counted in the computation of representation? Are they men? Then make them citizens and let them vote. Are they property? The very houses of Philadelphia alone are worth more than all the wretched slaves that are driven to toil in the rice fields of South Carolina. I had rather submit myself to a tax to buy up all the Negroes in the United States and give them mandamus than to saddle posterity with such a nefarious practice in this Constitution. I will never concur to upholding domestic slavery. It is a curse of heaven. If we cannot be reconciled on this issue, let us take friendly leave of each other and go our separate ways.

KING: Mr. Chairman, I also object to the inclusion of slaves in representation. It appears now that the importation of slaves will not be prohibited for at least another 20 years. Is this fair? Shall one part of the United States be bound to defend another, even though the second part continually endangers itself by increasing its slave population? The people of the Northern states will never be reconciled to this.

PINCKNEY: Mr. Chairman, I would like to move that the phrase "three-fifths" be removed entirely and that blacks should have full representation. The blacks are nothing more nor less than the peasantry of the southern states. They are just as productive as Northern laborers, adding to the wealth and strength of the nation. It is only simple justice that they should be equally represented in the general government.

PATTERSON: I would like to ask the speaker how he can suggest blacks be counted for equal representation when they are not allowed to vote?

WILLIAMSON: Mr. Chairman, as a resident of a slave state, I am opposed to slavery both in opinion and in practice. Nevertheless, I think that the two sectors would be far better uniting than going their separate ways.

WILSON: Mr. Chairman, call the question on the motion that slaves count as three-fifths of a person in the House of Representatives.

WASHINGTON: All in favor?

THE VAST MAJORITY: Aye.

WASHINGTON: Opposed?

MORRIS AND A FEW OTHERS: Nay.

GERRY: Mr. Chairman, before we adjourn, there is one final item I believe we should consider. I believe the right to trial by jury should be secured somewhere within this document.

MASON: Mr. Chairman, I would go even further. I think the entire Constitution should be prefaced by a Bill of Rights, comparable to the Declaration of Rights we have in Virginia. Whether we recognize it or not, the people fear central government. A set of guarantees limiting power has already been incorporated into the state constitutions. A similar enumeration here would allay public fears. Such a declaration could be drawn up within a few hours.

PINCKNEY: Mr. Chairman, I have already outlined such a proposal, which I would like to put before this convention. A Bill of Rights should include the following:

The writ of Habeas Corpus shall not be suspended, except on the most pressing occasions.

The liberty of the press shall be inviolable.

The military shall always be subordinate to the civil power.

No soldier shall be quartered in any private house in time of peace without consent of the owner.

No religious test shall be annexed to any oath of office administered under the authority of the United States.

GERRY: Mr. Chairman, I move we appoint a committee to prepare a Bill of Rights, using the suggestions set forth by Mr. Mason and Mr. Pinckney.

MASON: Seconded.

SHERMAN: Mr. Chairman, I am very much in favor of securing the rights of the people, but I wonder if such an inclusion is necessary. The Declarations of Rights of the states are not repealed by this Constitution. I view this Constitution as an assignment of limited powers. I believe the Senate and the Assembly can be trusted in these matters.

MADISON: I would like to concur with Mr. Sherman. Although several points suggested by Mr. Pinckney can be woven into the fabric of the document, I do not favor a separate list of prohibitions.

This Constitution is an enumeration of powers granted to the government by a free people. It assumes the people already hold a reservoir of inalienable rights. The proposals of Mr. Mason and

Mr. Gerry, on the contrary, presume that the government already holds the power and only grants rights to the people under specific dispensations. Once a few rights are granted, the question will inevitably arise whether others must be enumerated as well. In the end, either the list must be lengthened indefinitely or else power will shift subtly to the government. The surest way to allow the people to retain their rights may be not to enumerate anything at all.

WILSON: Call the question, Mr. Chairman.

WASHINGTON: On Mr. Mason's motion to appoint a committee to draw up a Bill of Rights. All in favor?

A FEW DELEGATES: Aye.

WASHINGTON: Opposed?

THE VAST MAJORITY: Nay.

WASHINGTON: The nays have it. Motion to adjourn?

HAMILTON: So moved.

PINCKNEY: Seconded.

WASHINGTON: All in favor?

ALL: Aye!

WASHINGTON: We shall convene tomorrow morning for a reading of the full document that is before us.

Act III, Scene 3

A reception at the home of Robert Morris.

The usual assemblage of attendees. GEORGE and MARTHA WASHINGTON again stand regally in the background. MRS. RITTENHOUSE, MRS. MORRIS, GOUVERNEUR MORRIS talk in the foreground.

MRS. MORRIS: Mr. Morris, I understand you gave a brilliant speech against slavery today.

MORRIS: My vows do not allow me to respond in detail, madam, so I will simply bask in your flattery.

RITTENHOUSE: It's a wretched business, isn't it, Mr. Morris?

MORRIS: Abominable, madam. It putrefies our shores. To my mind it is reason enough to abort our union.

RITTENHOUSE: So why is the convention accepting it?

MORRIS: Too many men of trade, madam, too many practitioners of compromise.

(HAMILTON approaches.)

RITTENHOUSE: Colonel Hamilton, I heard you had returned.

HAMILTON: I could not stay away, madam. I am now the entire New York delegation.

MORRIS: You represent them better than three men, Alex.

MRS. MORRIS: Yes, what's your opinion on this slavery question, Colonel Hamilton?

HAMILTON: It is an abomination, but we must live with it. If the two sections do not unite now, we will be as flint and powder. We will be at war with each other within ten years.

RITTENHOUSE: I supposed if one of us could pick up and move to the antipodes, it would be much easier, wouldn't it?

HAMILTON: We will live cheek-by-jowl no matter what the resolution of this issue. We must have union first and solve our differences later.

MORRIS: Colonel Hamilton, I must disagree although this is not the proper place.

HAMILTON: Yes, Gouverneur, I was just going over to the inn and thought you might want to join me.

MORRIS: To collect that steak dinner you owe me?

HAMILTON: I don't recall owing you any dinner, Gouverneur.

MORRIS: You will in a minute, Colonel Hamilton.

RITTENHOUSE: Is there something we're supposed to understand here, Mr. Morris?

MORRIS: Just a little exercise in the aristocratic spirit, madam. Colonel Hamilton has wagered that I will approach General Washington, clap him on the back, and ask how he is feeling tonight.

RITTENHOUSE: In public?

MORRIS: Where else, madam?

MRS. MORRIS: I don't think the General will tolerate that kind of behavior, Mr. Morris.

MORRIS: We shall see, madam.

MRS. MORRIS: Mr. Morris -

(Morris strides across the room, approaches Washington, and puts his arm around his shoulder.)

MORRIS: Good evening, General. It certainly is good to see you looking so well tonight.

(Washington stiffens, removes the arm from his shoulder, and gives him a long, withering look. Morris shrinks away, retreating slowly and apologetically, finally skulking out of the room.)

RITTENHOUSE: That certainly didn't go over very well, did it, Colonel Hamilton?

HAMILTON: Good ladies, will you promise me one thing? Don't ever let the General know of my part in this unfortunate affair.

Act III, Scene 4

The City Tavern, September 16, 1787

WILSON and MADISON sit alone.

WILSON: Jemmy - may I call you that? - I want to ask if you could work with me during the ratification in Philadelphia. I wrote a great deal during the British controversy but the people have grown tired of me.

MADISON: James, I'd love to but Alex and I have to work plans together. We're publishing a series of letters to the people of the State of New York defending the document.

WILSON: Can you send me copies? I can have them printed here as well. They should be published everywhere in fact.

MADISON: That's a good idea.

WILSON: You and Alex make a formidable team when you're in harness together - not that you always agree.

MADISON: Checks and balances.

WILSON: Yes, the wisdom of the convention. Tell me, what do you see as our strategy for ratification?

MADISON: We must move quickly before the opposition can organize itself. People are already criticizing the document without having seen it.

WILSON: What kind of arguments will they make?

MADISON: Oh, anything and everything. The government is too strong, it's too weak, there are too many Senators, there are too few. Every conceivable possibility will be weighed against the few tangibilities we have to offer.

WILSON: It's an extraordinary thing, isn't it, this business of self-government. Such a yearning for it and yet such a fear of it as well.

MADISON: It will take time.

WILSON: It's a marvelous time to be living, though, isn't it? I mean here you are, what, 35 years old -

MADISON: Thirty-six.

WILSON: You probably don't even remember what it was like back in '69, before the French War started. We were more British than the British themselves, the most content of all English subjects. Then the war began and suddenly people found themselves living things they'd only read in history books.

MADISON: I remember most of it.

WILSON: The age of republican government - it will produce wonders never imagined.

MADISON: It may produce horrors never imagined as well.

WILSON: You have a very skeptical turn of mind, don't you, Mr. Madison?

MADISON: I shouldn't be so pessimistic. I admit there is great promise. Yet the dreary history of republican failure makes it hard to be too confident.
WILSON: You do believe people in this country have

Republican virtue, don't you?

MADISON: As much as any other people in history, I suppose.

WILSON: And if our experiment succeeds, won't Europe have to follow? Won't the age of crowned heads soon be forgotten?

MADISON: The era of kings and princes has ended before, only to be replaced by something worse.

WILSON: You know, Mr Madison, sometimes I think you know too much history. In this country it may be just as important to forget the past as to remember it.

MADISON: I'm sorry, James. I may be more hopeful than I dare admit. We may not answer the question as to whether men are capable of governing themselves, but at least we have raised it.

WILSON: Oh, we've done much better than that, Mr. Madison, much better. Don't you think that one hundred years from now - two hundred years from now – in Europe, in Russia, maybe even the Empires of the East, people will look back and say something extraordinary happened in Philadelphia this summer?

MADISON: It's possible, James. And I sincerely hope its' true.

WILSON: So how's our friend Gouverneur doing?

MADISON: He has recovered from his embarrassment and is working on the committee on style. I believe they report tomorrow morning.

WILSON: Well, then, you see? Even our friend Gouverneur is

back on board. So, (toasts), here's to the era of self-government. Long may it endure.

MADISON: (Toasts back.) Far may it prevail.

Act III, Scene 5

Independence Hall, September 17, 1787

The full convention is assembled.

DOCTOR JOHNSON: Mr. Chairman, you now have before you the final draft of the Constitution. The committee has added a preface. In deference to Mr. Morris, who has composed it, we would ask that he read it.

MORRIS: "We the People of the United States, in order to form a more perfect union, establish justice, insure domestic tranquility, provide for the common defense, promote the general welfare, and secure the blessings of liberty for ourselves and our posterity, do hereby ordain and establish this Constitution of the United States of America."

      (A scattering of applause that swells to a crescendo, then dies down.)

WILSON: Motion to adopt the Constitution as written, Mr. Chairman.

HAMILTON: Seconded.

WASHINGTON: All in favor?

ALL: (Loudly) Aye.

      (There is a moment of awe as the delegates realize what they have accomplished.)

WASHINGTON: Gentlemen, before the delegates are asked to sign the document, several members have indicated they do not intend to sign this Constitution and have asked to address the convention.

RANDOLPH: Mr. Chairman, it is with great trepidation that I stand before you today. The plan as adopted is not that far distant from the one I proposed four months ago. I realize I may be making the most awful mistake of my life, yet I find I cannot sign this document for fear it will be rejected by the people. Nine states will not ratify it and the result will be utter confusion and despair.

MASON: Mr. Chairman, I must join Governor Randolph in refusing to sign. This constitution has been formed without the knowledge of the people. It will end either in a monarchy or a tyrannical aristocracy. I find the implied sanctions of slavery intolerable. I believe Congress and the states must be allowed to amend this document or we must hold another convention.

PINCKNEY: Mr. Chairman, these declarations at the close of this important scene give the moment a peculiar solemnity. There are several parts of this Constitution that I find unacceptable - particularly the contemptibly weak dependency of the executive and the reduced representation of slaves. Yet I cannot accept the suggestion that we call another convention. Constitutional conventions are awesome events and ought not to be degraded by needless repetition.

HAMILTON: Mr. Chairman, may I also express my fervent anxiety that every member sign this Constitution. Let me remind you that no man's ideas were more remote than my own from the document we now have before us. Yet is it possible for any man, no matter what his particular view, to hesitate further in the face of the anarchy and convulsions that will attend if the nation does not accept our effort?

GERRY: Mr. Chairman, I am sorry but I must also express my refusal to sign. I still find several aspects objectionable. The power of the House to conceal its journals, the three-fifths allocation for blacks, the fact that my own state of Massachusetts does not have her due share of representation - all are insurmountable. In my own state, all parties will oppose this document, which can only lead to civil war. I see no better solution than to call a second convention and begin again.

FRANKLIN: Mr. Chairman, I have prepared some remarks but in deference to age, I would ask that Mr. Wilson read them for me.

WILSON: (reading) "Mr. Chairman, I confess that there are several parts of this Constitution of which I do not at present approve, but I am not sure I will never approve them. For having lived a long time, I have experienced many instances of being obliged to change my opinion on important subjects. It is for this reason that, the older I grow, the more apt I am to doubt my own judgment and pay more respect to the judgment of others.

"Sir, I agree to this Constitution with all its faults, if they be such, because I think a general government is necessary for us. There is no form of government but what may be a blessing to the people if well administered, and no form that cannot end in despotism if the people shall become corrupted. Therefore I doubt whether any other convention we may obtain can make a better Constitution.

"For when you assemble . . .."

FRANKLIN: (rises, takes his notes from Wilson, and finishes himself). For when you assemble a number of men to have the advantage of their joint wisdom, you inevitably bring with them all their prejudices, passions, errors, and selfish views. Can a perfect production ever be expected from such an assembly? I doubt it. It therefore astonishes me, Sir, to find this system approaching so near perfection as it does now. Thus, I consent to this Constitution because I expect none better, and because I am not sure that it is not the best.

I cannot help expressing as well, Sir, a wish that every member of the Convention, on this occasion, would doubt a little his own infallibility, and make manifest our unanimity by putting his name on this instrument. If this cannot be done, then I would propose that the document be closed as follows: "Done in convention by the unanimous consent of the *States* present the 17th of September, 1787."

HAMILTON: Seconded.

WASHINGTON: All in favor of Dr. Franklin's motion?

ALL: Aye.

(The delegates come forward to sign the Constitution. Mason, Randolph, and Gerry stand conspicuously apart. After signing, Dr. Franklin moves downstage and comments to a few members around him.)

FRANKLIN: Gentlemen, oft have I heard that painters in their art experience great difficulty in distinguishing between a rising and setting sun. Time and again during the course of our deliberations, I have gazed upon yonder sun carved on the back of the President's chair and wondered whether its orb were rising or setting. Yet now, at last, in the culmination of our efforts, I have the happiness to know that what we are looking upon is a rising, not a setting, sun.

(As the convention breaks up, MRS. HOUSE rushes onstage.)

MRS. HOUSE: Dr. Franklin! Dr. Franklin! What kind of government have you given us, Dr. Franklin?

FRANKLIN: A republic, madam! (Turns to audience.) If *you* can keep it!